Desiree Lee presents

PASS THE MUSTARD SEED

"It's our faith that moves mountains, not our hands."

You've come too far to give up now.

12-30-15

ISBN-13: 978-1502958709

This book includes information from many sources and personal experiences. It is intended to be used as a guide and a resource for its readers and is not intended to replace or substitute professional counseling or therapy where necessary. The publisher and author do not claim any responsibility or liability, directly or indirectly, for information or advice presented. While accuracy and completeness of the material, we claim no responsibility for potential inaccuracies, omissions, incompleteness, error, or inconsistencies.

For more information, contact I Am Desiree Lee, LLC, at www.DLeeInspires.com or via email at d.lee7211@gmail.com

Ordering Information

Quantity Sales: Special discounts are available on quantity purchases by U.S. Trade Bookstores, Wholesalers, Corporations, Non-Profit Organizations, Associations and Others. For further details, contact publisher I Am Desiree Lee LLC at email address above.

Cover design by I Am Desiree Lee, LLC

Website: www.DLeeInspires.com | Email: d.lee7211@gmail.com |
Facebook: dleeinspires | Twitter: dleeinspires | Instagram: dleeinspires

Whatever your 100% looks like, give it!
I dedicate this book to "YOU", the reader.
You are much stronger than you think.

ACKNOWLEDGEMENTS

In spite of my past mistakes, I am tremendously grateful that God hasn't given up on me. That He has entrusted me (a willing vessel) to birth the vision of PASS THE MUSTARD, to remind others that it is our faith that pleases Him. Thank you God!

To my parents, who love and support me without condition; Thank you both for uplifting me and being a listening ear when I need you the most.

My mentors, family, and friends who have pushed me along the way, to get this book completed. You all play an intricate part in my development.

To the featured contributing authors, you all have blessed me beyond measure. Your tenacity towards your triumph is phenomenal and your transparency will be greatly appreciated to those who read your stories. I am certain that the mustard seeds passed will uplift the readers in their time of need, to overcome life's most difficult barriers. Thank you all for not giving up while going through.

DEAR READER,

There is something to be said about passing the mustard seed. I remember the day I met Ms. Desiree Lee. A stunningly beautiful woman, with her mother in the neighborhood nail salon.

As a busy Mom, I was there for a regular visit, taking time to exhale and enjoying "ME" time. As she walked in there was something different about Desiree's spirit. She was searching inwardly.

I simply spoke to her affirming what God said and birthed in Desiree from the beginning. She held onto the mustard seeds, as they begin to grow and blossom within her. Nurtured and watered by the inspiration of others, you are now seeing the harvest from a tiny mustard seed. I am honored to be a part of this young woman's journey.

Desiree, may God continue to expand and enlarge your territory in ways you would have never imagined.

With Love,

Jestacia Jones

"The Lady with the Mustard Seed"

TABLE OF CONTENTS

"The tiny seed knew that in order to grow, it needed to be dropped in dirt, covered in darkness, and struggle to reach the light.

Desiree Lee

Founder & Creator of 10 City Prison Prevention Tour | Best Selling Author | Inspirational Speaker | Philanthropist | Author Workshop Facilitator
Website: www.DLeeInspires.com | Email: d.lee7211@gmail.com |
Facebook: dleeinspires | Twitter: dleeinspires | Instagram: dleeinspires

DLEE INSPIRES LLC

Desiree Lee
"Passing the Mustard Seed: Introduction"

You may have faced many defeats, but you must not be defeated. Opportunities are usually disguised as impossible situations. Once we've decided to shift our minds towards how God see's it; then and only then our impossible transforms into IM-POSSIBLE.

Like many, there was a time during my journey where I found myself in dark place. It was so dark and there was not a single glimpse of light, so I thought. You may have read in my first book ***INMATE 1142980: "The Desiree Lee Story"*** of my dark place experience. This dark place stemmed from making several attempts to gain employment, an apartment, go to college, along with a list of other limitations that I've encountered with a criminal background. Confronted with the daunting words of, "I am sorry ma'am, but we can't accept anyone with a criminal background." Every option was no longer a possibility. I was alone, scared, and doubtful. Not knowing what else to do until the day I met the lady with the mustard seed, Jestacia Jones.

On this day, "faith" became real to me. She poured a few mustard seeds inside of my hand from the small jar in her purse. The tiny seed was a reminder of the amount of faith God requires us to have. Realizing that sometimes our problems stack up so high, that they become our mountains. In the Bible, Matthew 17:20 NIV *"Truly I tell you, if you have faith as small as a mustard seed, you can say to this mountain, 'Move from here to there,' and it will move. Nothing is impossible for you."* Therefore, open your mouth and speak to every mountain that is hindering you from reaching greater heights, and tell your mountains to MOVE! Then and only then, nothing is no longer impossible. Ah-ha! I finally get it. It's not your environment that dictates your success, it's your mind.

With this scripture in mind, I've made a conscious decision to believe in the possible, just one last time. In as little as thirty days later, I met with Jestacia and shared my praise report. After my excitement settled, Jestacia mentioned of her dark place experience. A lady during her time of need, poured in her hand a tiny mustard seed, and spoke life over her life. With gratitude I replied, "Thank you for not giving up while you were going through your darkest moment, because my life was depending on your faith to persevere."

There are times when we are going through some of the most trying times in our lives that it seems as if the world is caving in on us. As if we are the only people who may be going through the roughest hardships, to the point where we want everyone to join in with our pity party. I want to inform you that even in the midst of the darkest place, you can't give up because there is someone who is depending on your faith. At God's appointed time, a lady gave a mustard seed to Jestacia. Jestacia gave a mustard seed to me. I am committed to continue passing the mustard seed, which was passed to me during one of the toughest times in my life. Igniting a domino effect of others pouring into others. It is my hope as a nation and worldwide, that one day we all will see the harvest from passing the mustard seed.

"The tiny seed knew that in order to grow, it needed to be dropped in dirt, covered in darkness, and struggle to reach the light."

–Desiree Lee

THE POWER OF THE DARK PLACE:

A farmer doesn't plant without knowing what harvest to expect. Whatever harvest is expected, the farmer plants the seeds desired. If you want an apple harvest, plant an apple seed. If you're expecting a bountiful pumpkin harvest, plant pumpkin seeds. And so on.

During my dark place experience, it was my expectation to overcome my life's most difficult barriers therefore, I had decided to plant my mustard seed right in the midst of doubt, fear, hurt, pain, and failure. What you are seeing today is the harvest from my mustard seed. Name your seed and in due season you shall reap a harvest, if you faint not.

Maybe you have either found yourself in the similar dark place or are currently there. I want you to know that you are not alone and you still have power in your choice. You have the choice to throw in the towel or use it to wipe the sweat off of your face. If you don't like your harvest, change your seed. So, GET UP & GROW!

Many of the authors featured in this book, found themselves at one time or another in a dark place until someone along their journey gave them a friendly reminder that they can plant again. By faith, we can now pass our mustard seed to you, as a reminder that NOTHING IS IMPOSSIBLE! You don't drown by falling in the water. You drown by staying there.

"The genius thing that we did was, we didn't give up." – Jay-Z

OUTSTANDING Jewelry™

Taliyah

Brianna

"If you put God's effort in your heart, if you want to do it, the impossible will be possible."

Brianna

"If you put your mind to it, pray, and God will bless you in many ways. So don't be scared to want help from God or people.

GOD LOVES YOU AND WILL BLESS YOU!"

Taliyah

Founders of Outbanding Jewelry | Young Entrepreneurs
Website: www.outbandingjewelry.com | Email: outbanding@gmail.com | Facebook:
Outbanding Jewelry | Instagram: Outbanding Jewelry

OUTBANDING JEWELRY

Brianna & Taliyah
"Receiving the Mustard Seed"

If there is one thing that is amazing, it is God's timing. One can never know when God will show up and move. It is only our job to be ready and obedient. This is a concept that many adults have yet to grasp, so imagine understanding this at only 12 years old.   Well, Taliyah Wright, an ambitious and bright 12 year old girl, saw an opportunity, took it and ran with it, dragging her 8 year old little sister, Brianna Roach, along with her for the ride.

These two girls had officially been sisters for only a few months. Taliyah's father, Roderic, married Brianna's mother, Naomi. While they considered each other sisters for many years, the girls found comfort in the joining of their two families. Naomi worked as a manager at an advertisement company while Roderic was jumpstarting his own business as a videographer and editor. On August 15, 2014, Roderic took his family to work with him so his daughters could hear his client, Desiree Lee, and her powerful story. Roderic and Naomi could tell the girls were moved, but they had no idea to what degree Desiree's story impacted them.

Taliyah was shocked at the idea that this woman could have succumbed to peer pressure from her friends that would lead her down such a terrible path. Taliyah, being in 7th grade, was at a time in her life when her friends seemed to be her world. She never fathomed that listening to them in the wrong situation could cost her as much as Desiree lost. Taliyah made a personal decision that she would find ways to occupy her time to prevent herself from getting so caught up in what school friends were doing. She would focus on something more positive.

Brianna on the other hand, heard Desiree recite Martin Luther King's inspiring statement

"If you can't fly, then you run, if you can't run, then you walk, if you can't walk, then you crawl. But whatever you do, you have to keep on moving."

Hearing Desiree recite those words through her tears stuck with Brianna and made her want to work hard and keep going on for greatness. Brianna noticed that both Roderic and her own father worked hard at their own businesses and she wanted to be as accomplished as they were.

When Taliyah went up to Desiree to have her book signed, Desiree sparked conversation with Taliyah explaining how you're never too young to make good decisions. Desiree asked,

"Well, do you have a business?"

Taliyah seized the opportunity and told her,

"Yes!" without hesitation.

Desiree asked her what kind of business she owned. Taliyah told Desiree that she made rubber band jewelry and sold it.

"Well, where's your business card? How can I buy some?" Desiree asked.

Most kids Taliyah's age probably would have said they didn't have any or feel discouraged. Taliyah however took that as a challenge. She ran to the car and got a piece of paper. She wrote down her name and her number along with the types of jewelry she made and their prices. She ran to give her information to Desiree in the parking lot as they were leaving the building. Again, when God moves you have to be ready and obedient.

Desiree was very impressed with Taliyah's quick wit and initiative. As God would have it, a lady named Kelly walked over to Desiree to tell her about a festival she was having in the area and offered an invitation to her. Desiree said she would join the festival, but only if Kelley sponsored a table to Taliyah as well. Desiree told Kelly all about the rubber band jewelry business that Taliyah has and how ambitious the young girl was. Kelly accepted and offered Taliyah a table, and with that, Outbanding Jewelry was born.

Taliyah immediately partnered with her younger sister, Brianna, to work on bracelets, charms, necklaces, and rings; they made everything that they could possibly make with rubber bands in preparation for this festival. The girls took what they loved doing and cultivated that into a business in a matter of weeks. People in their family saw what they were doing and wanted to support them and before they could even make it to the festival they were already bringing in a profit.

Their parents supported their vision too. Roderic immediately created graphics and visuals for them. He did a photo shoot for them, showing off their jewelry. Naomi managed their day to day activities and opened up various social media outlets for them to display their jewelry on. The girls put in long hours making jewelry, and enlisted the help of their friends too. This really became a family business. The festival was such a success that they were invited to more festivals and asked to vendor at more events. Desiree took them with her around town to speak to other children about the good decisions they made. This excited the girls, especially Taliyah. She loved sharing their story with other kids. The idea of traveling and inspiring someone to make a good decision to help their life for the better motivated her.

As they continued with the festivals, Outbanding proved to be a lot of hard work. After homework was done they had to make sure they continued to make enough jewelry for each new event. As people ordered more custom jewelry, they had to make sure it was done just right. Their parents stayed on them to keep them focused. Many days they would have just rather gone outside to play. Taliyah especially wanted to take time out to hang with her friends, but whenever she thought about being a possible example for other kids, it gave her the boost she needed to get her work done.

Taliyah and Brianna both want to see Outbanding Jewelry reach its full potential. Even though the girl's motivation and goals for the business are different, they each know that it will take continued hard work and effort to make Outbanding a successful business. Taliyah would love to continue to work Outbanding with a goal for it to pay her way through college. She also wants to work other jobs through school in order to know what it's like to have a boss so that she can learn to be a good boss herself. Brianna would love to see Outbanding grow and be her full time career so that she can pass it down to her children when they are her age. Both girls would love to grow Outbanding Jewelry into something that can expand beyond retail and into other fields such as motivational speaking and entertainment.

In order for the girls to reach this and other goals, their parents are very aware that it will take their continued support. They plan to continue to push their girls and keep them focused on new and fresh ideas for their business. They will also work to teach them to maintain a balance between work and school responsibilities, all while keeping them fun loving children. The girls work to try and keep business fun by making jewelry with their friends and having parties and sleep overs while they create new innovative products. Naomi and Roderic also know the importance of keeping their girls surrounded by friends and family that can show them the importance of creativity and entrepreneurship.

In addition to all the goals, lessons, and responsibilities that these girls are learning so young to balance, the most important thing Outbanding is teaching them is how God honors and blesses faith and hard work. The girls include their business and their accomplishments in their prayers daily. They have asked their church to support and pray for them and all their endeavors. Taliyah and Brianna have learned at an early age, that when you are blessed, you must share your testimony so that you can be a blessing to others. If people can see how God blesses them, maybe people will believe that He will bless them too, and they can be encouraged through their success. They have not only heard, but they have experienced that God is no respecter of a person, no matter their age. If you are ready and obedient when God presents his opportunity, then there is no limit to how high you can reach. He will even bless a 12 and 8 year old with a vision!

The girls are very aware that God has shown them many things. From Brianna's words

"If you put God's effort in your heart, if you want to do it, the impossible will be possible."

And as Taliyah eloquently puts it,

"If you put your mind to it, pray, and God will bless you in many ways. So don't be scared to want help from God or people. GOD LOVES YOU AND WILL BLESS YOU!"

"Be the change you want to see."

Christa "K Joy" Williams

Radio Executive Producer & Host | Beauty Care Specialist | Public Figure
Website: www.thebeautyessentialsshow.com |
Email: Email:beautyessentialsbraodcast@gmail.com |
Facebook: The Beauty Essentials Show | Twitter: @b_essentials4u |
Instagram: thebeautyessentials | YouTube: Christa Williams Beauty Essentials

THE BEAUTY ESSENTIALS SHOW

Christa "K Joy" Williams

"The Power of My Mustard Seed: Determination"

Never in a million years, did I think radio broadcasting would be the mouthpiece of my vision. All it took was my deepest want, faith and one small phrase. Before I knew it, placed before me was my ministry behind the radio microphone and I have been in love with my new career ever since.

Before I began my unexpected radio broadcasting career I was a former educator from 2007-2012 in Augusta, Georgia. At first, I was apprehensive of becoming a teacher, but I decided to give it a try. My first year was tough because of being blinded sided by the ins and outs of the school system and how things functioned. I had to educate myself how to teach my students as people and as a group, how to set up my classroom for learning according to the students' learning abilities and manage paperwork of our annual curriculum mandated by the county. Not to mention be a mother, father, counselor, nurse, and mentor to my students because of their various personalities and home lifestyles. So just imagine how I was feeling at the end of every work day. Well, needless to say I overcame my educator obstacles and found my passion for teaching, well, at least I thought I did. As the second year of my teaching career passed me by, I began enjoying the world of teaching. Developing relationships with the students and their parents, creating an intriguing atmosphere for learning and becoming a family with my grade level co-workers. Along my educator journey, I just felt like something was missing in my life but I just couldn't put my finger on it. So I decided to dismiss the idea and continue on with life.

In the mist of everything that was occurring in my life, a close relative introduced me to the beauty industry because she felt my personality and my open mindset was the key to me becoming successful in this billion dollar company with a household name attached to it. She introduced me to one of the top business women in the history of this billion dollar company. I was in complete amazement when I met this iconic woman. She was the "crème' de la crème" of her time and then some. As we engaged in conversation about how she teaches people on skin care and how she help others to become not only great business men and women, but an inspiration to all. Her story inspired me to become a beauty care consultant with the company. Along with the aspirations of wanting to help people to not only view and experience magnitude about themselves, but evolve into an inspirational testimony for the world. When I left her office, my outlook on life itself and my want and need to become affiliated with this encouraging movement, became the spark that lit my burning passion for what God had aligned for my future.

One morning before our students arrived at school, I was conversing with my co-worker, whom I was very close to, about the new curriculum that we had to teach our students. Also, the possibility that some of the teachers would be changing grade levels during the school year and other stressful factors that would take place inside of our school. Needless to say, the frustrations of teaching really began to set in and I was still having all these mixed emotions of my life being a blur and meaningless. As I continued my chat with my colleague, I had an epiphany. I remember saying to her, "I don't see myself teaching for thirty years. I feel like my life has more purpose than just THIS." Now don't get me wrong I loved the students and the parents and where I taught. I just did not love the business side of teaching and the sudden and unnecessary changes the administration and the county were putting on teachers. For days, I replayed the conversation I experienced with the woman I met earlier and me stating that small phrase changed my entire mindset on becoming more than just living a cookie cutter lifestyle. In May 2012, my life took a drastic 180 degree turn from being a new mother and employed with great benefits to unemployed and a stay at home mother. I found myself empty, confused and insignificant. During my time frame of unemployment, I did find various ways to bring in sources of income for the household. I found myself going back into retail making minimum wage and working long hours. Three months later I quit that job. I tried auto sales which lasts about three months due to the management's behaviors towards specific sale consultants so, I quit that job. Finally, I did direct sales which I absolutely loved, however, people who were close to me couldn't understand the business opportunities behind it and advice was given to me not to pursue it. I didn't quit this one, I just slowed down on my progress because of my aspirations for beauty, fashion and health. At this point, I have gone through so much in my life and felt like I have not accomplished a thing so far. The determination to find something that would be a great fit for Christa was my mission and in the summer of 2013, that is exactly what happened.

I will never forget this day as long as I live. It was a warm partly cloudy day of June 2013 and I decided to drive around the Aiken/Augusta area to clear my mind and plan my next moves on what to do with my life. As I thought to myself, I began turning the radio dial in my car and a local radio station was advertising for sales associates. So I thought to myself "hey, why not give this a shot" and began writing the information on an old receipt from my purse. I called the number from the receipt to show interest in the sales associate opportunity. From there, I was given information on the date, time and meeting place for orientation. I made it my business to present in my best professional attire and to have my résumé that listed my experiences from retail management to education. As I walked into the orientation meeting, there were only two of us that responded to the radio advertisement. I thought to myself "is this for me? Will this be a prosperous career for my daughter and me?" So many questions where playing in my head, but I just embraced the opportunity to stay humble and open-minded. The management team of the radio station were highly impressed by my work experiences, so they decided to hire me as a member of the sales team. Following the orientation, I along with the other candidate, began our sales training and began my new job as a sales associate in radio broadcasting. Over time, I began to enjoy my new radio career because of the unique work environment. Never in my years of employment have I experienced being among other staff members that have your best interest at heart. This gave me all the more reason to stay and make the opportunity work for my good. On a constant basis I displayed my efforts of becoming a more enhanced sales associate and asked the general manager for guidance on improving my sales techniques. I continued to work diligently on establishing my client list via telephone and email in hopes of producing income for my household since my source of income was commission based. So I needed to work extra hard to meet the goals of becoming a successful sales team member. I accomplished a small number of sales here and there, but not an adequate amount to sustain for my daughter and me. I began to speculate, yet again, why I was positioned in my current situation. Unaware that my life would experience another level of greatness, I continued to remain enduring, content and humble in this test God placed before me.

As I was working a typical day at the office, the general manager called me into office. He asked me how I was doing financially. I was honest with him and I shared with him my unstable financial situation in detail. He said to me he saw how dedicated and diligent I was with my work. So, he offered me a salary based position to become the office manager at the radio station because they were in need of someone to administer the operations of the office. What a breakthrough this was for my daughter and me! I gladly accepted the promotion and began working in my new position the next day. The fact I was more of a team player and not looking for ways of being self-seeking in the office proved to the general manager I took my job seriously. The general manager saw more in me than I saw in myself.

In addition, I displayed so much energy into becoming a better asset for the station. As my voyage into the radio business took off from a sales associate to the office manager, I kept a positive spirit and an open mindset to the endless opportunities. But guess what, God was not finished with his plan for me all because of the power of the tongue and my deepest belief in my vision. One morning on my way to the office, I was listening to one of the announcers from our station discuss a topic on health. And I thought to myself "it would be awesome if they had a broadcast on fashion and beauty". When I arrived to the office the general manager needed to speak with me. He said for a long time he has wanted to launch a new radio show about fashion and beauty but he couldn't find the right person to fulfill the vision he had for the station. With a pause, he looked me in my eyes and asked if I would like to host a beauty radio show. My jaws dropped and I burst into tears of joy, I was speechless and gladly accepted this great opportunity with no hesitations. He told me I had 3 weeks to prep for the show which included creating a name for the broadcast and format according to the talk show time clock. My launch date was Saturday, September 6, 2013 at 10 AM EST and The Beauty Essentials Show was born.

Since I began my career change from education to radio broadcasting I have embraced various opportunities that found me. I knew in my spirit that my broadcast would become bigger than what it is now. The more I envisioned and believed in my greatness, the more opportunities have allowed me to excel to the next level in my mission to aid individuals on transforming themselves from ordinary into extraordinary people. I spoke my desires and passion into existence not knowing the journey I was going to take to get to where I am now. My experiences are the testimonies I can share with my listeners and they can relate to what I am giving out, especially hot topic issues. I am a firm believer of going after what you wish for and never giving up no matter what life throws at you. I wanted to share my story with you on how the power of the tongue is greater than voicing you thoughts into the universe. It's truly believing in them and knowing it will evolve into reality.

As you walk into your vision, I would like to share some great tips on becoming better than you aspire to be. Here are 7 principles you can implement to grow your mustard seed and become successful with life itself.

1. ***Know your passion and believe in it!*** Visualize what you want your dreams to look like as the end results. The more you become one with your vision with time it will evolve into reality.

2. ***Never give up!*** No matter what is going in your life or who discourages you, stay focused and continue to breathe life into your dreams.

3. ***Open your mind, body and soul to any and all positive energies.*** Meditation is a great habit to implement into your morning and nightly routine. It will stimulate your mind to think on an elevated and positive level.

4. ***Feed your mind Positive thoughts.*** Read any forms of inspirational literature or listen to positive or soothing music in the morning, afternoon and evening. Remember, you are what you think!

5. ***Network, Network, Network!*** Put yourself in a position to grow. You will not be able excel if you are not meeting people. Attend various business and social events in your area. Pass out your business cards and just mingle! Use social media to your advantage. Being in the social media arena is an asset to your vision. Facebook, Instagram and Twitter are great tools for social media networking.

6. ***Refrain from sharing your vision with everyone.*** The only person that needs to know your business ideas, aspirations and vision is you!

7. ***Find time for your vision and work on them daily.*** Whether it is 15 minutes or an hour schedule an allotted time for your vision and be consistent!

I pray that my story and principles will inspire you to achieve great and mighty ventures in your lifetime. My mission in life is to assist individuals to maximize their potential for greatness as visionaries. Therefore, I am passing my mustard seed of faith, desire and position to all who receive this seed. Remember, you are more than what you are now and extraordinary beyond your wildest dreams.

*"Accept the journey, commit to growth, and
be honest with who you are. Because I believe in YOU!"*

Nedra Buckmire

Co-Pastor | Mentor | Certified Professional Life Coach | Workshop Facilitator
Email: nbuck390@gmail.com | Facebook: Nedra Buckmire | Twitter: @nbuck390

REWRITING YOUR FUTURE

Nedra L. Buckmire
"The Mustard Seed of Courage"

I don't believe that anyone decisively seeks to be average. Unfortunately, certain circumstances and situations that life provokes can impede a person from progression. Critical incidents such as divorce or a traumatic experience can propel a person into a tail spin of uncertainty and halt life's progress. Dwelling in a place of immobility is like attempting to drive a car without an engine. Everything else is present and functioning in the car but without the engine, it's certain the car will go nowhere. I firmly believe and have validated through my own life's experience that every day can be a fresh start towards a new beginning. I can earnestly profess this perspective hasn't always been part of my life's journey. In the past, I viewed myself as a major underachiever especially in my adolescent and young adult years. As I reflect on my childhood and young adult life, I simply existed. I didn't have a desired path or chartered course to navigate. My actions weren't ordered or deliberate. I did what I thought was best and needed at the moment. I trust there are countless people that can relate to my story. I had no vision, no plan, and no passion. I was set on a course to live an undistinguished life and future. I followed in the footsteps of my mother and discovered I was gifted as an Administrative Assistant. I'd like to share three areas that helped me understand facing who I was, accepting my journey towards wholeness and my commitment to grow enabled me to ignite my purpose and passion and ultimately rewrite my future.

1. Be Honest With Who You Are

It's often difficult to face the truth, especially when it's not the reality you anticipated. If you allow the people in your life to provide raw honest feedback, you can grow but only if you have the maturity to accept what's imparted. Facing the real you, will be the first step in altering your current course and rewriting your desired future. I had to face my truth – the good, the bad and the ugly. I was employed, married with children but no higher education other than high school and a one-year secretarial program to my credit. However, there were a number of personal issues that plagued my life. The issues of my past caused low self-esteem, no-confidence, and a marred self-image because of sexual abuse. Yet, I functioned with all of this baggage for a good portion of my life without people knowing my hidden internal struggles. These areas were so much a part of me that I mastered functioning from my dysfunctions; or so I thought. Even though life's situations opened the door to many of these areas, I determined that the doors would be identified and each entry way be closed. I had to earnestly see myself for where I was, for who I had become and declare a change was critically necessary. If you are searching for truth and wholeness, know it's possible but not without a fight. Once you identify your current truth, whether it's emotional hurt or abuse, it's no longer obscure. When issues are not identified and readily dealt with, they remain in the dark and can seem vague and unreachable. Once issues are identified, they are uncovered and no longer possess the power of silence or uncertainty. My faith in God was and is the empowering force that enabled me to face my issues and be honest with myself so that I could begin my journey to being whole. Being honest with where you are, can inspire a cathartic release towards liberty. This same honesty prompted the discovery of the *real* me. As a believer in Christ, I had to see myself as God created me – *in His image and His likeness.* It was imperative that I believed I was more than every negative, shameful and hurtful experience I lived through including the nurturing I didn't receive. I had to face the person in the mirror and no longer hide behind an invisible mask of shame. God's love and His word empowered me to begin a journey with honesty, courage and resilience.

2. Accept the Journey

Once you've marshaled the courage to face whatever has crippled and the negatively impacted your life, you can't remain in a state of knowing you must walk out the process. By accepting the process, you're saying yes to your journey and to the authentic you. When the journey to wholeness is accepted, know it will be an arduous one but absolutely necessary. My path was tough because I had to grapple with the pain of the past in order to embrace my desired future. I didn't know the depth of where my process of restoration would take me but I was ready to move from emotional dysfunction and mere existence to becoming whole and thriving with purpose fueling my life. Accepting the journey is only half the battle; walking it out to the end is vital. I took comfort knowing I wasn't alone but God's presence enabled me every step of the way. His grace covered and saturated me as I endured every memory that invaded my heart and mind. When it was hurtful, I trusted God. When I didn't believe I could survive the barrage of memories, I trusted God. When I was overwhelmed, I trusted God. I faced my fears; I named my dysfunctional issues; and I became triumphant over the oppressions that held me in an unfruitful, immobile place. Entering and accepting this journey caused me to face certain pain but the victory was well worth the discomfort. It proved to be an emotional psychological rollercoaster, but I didn't give up. I wanted to be free. During the process, I wanted to retreat to cease the vivid memories from my past that permeated my thoughts and dreams. However, in order to be free perseverance was mandatory. Many people are halted at this point in the journey because in order to walk through to wholeness one must deal with the ugly things that initially opened the door to brokenness. If you are in this place, I admonish you to press forward and don't settle for anything less than 100% victory. Remember, you can't overcome what you deny. You will face a few defining moments along the way where you must make a definitive decision. Please make the decision based upon where you desire to be and not what you are currently experiencing. By your actions, you are building confidence, strength and hope. With God's help, you are more than able to finish strong.

3. Commit to Growth

After walking through to wholeness, a passion was awakened within me to empower others that find themselves stunted, stuck and unable to move from a place of emotional or life's challenges. I've often heard the statement - *your mess will become your ministry* or *your mess will become your message*. Either way when you are free, you desire others to be free also. You become emboldened to awaken another from their conflict. Being free helps you to see with a clearer, uncluttered perspective. When a person is hindered or halted with emotional barriers and wounds, it's very difficult to function or minister from a healthy place. They will see as they are and not necessarily as any given situation presents itself. After experiencing the transforming power of the almighty God in my life, I knew I had to empower others to be free. I begin to experience an awakening in my aspirations to be something greater than what I had ever experienced. My newly-awakened passions were the direct result of believing and applying the Word of God to my life. My faith coupled with the word of God caused a transformation in how I saw myself, believed in my ability and walked out the word in truth. I believed what the word of God said I could do and be. God allowed divine connections to enter my life and make indelible marks shaping a woman for purpose and destiny. God assigned men and women to speak words of life, affirmation, inspiration and encouragement while challenging me to increase my capacity. No one achieves greatness alone. God has specifically purposed individuals that will provoke and propel you towards the next step in your destiny. My future is being rewritten before my eyes. I am a willing participant and I'm in pursuit of my destiny. It's not something that happened to me. It's something that happened within me. When the fire of purpose is ignited within, it will fuel passions and motivate you to achieve great things. Unlike previously in my life where I just existed, I now make deliberate decisions by setting goals to further my insatiable desire to grow. Whatever your priority, it will receive the majority of your time and efforts.

After completing my undergrad as an adult, married with children and at the time a newly-formed ministry, I made the commitment in what seemed like chaos to become a life-time learner. Whether in a classroom, on-line course, reading a book or poetry. I must continually grow. I was blessed to graduate Summa Cum Laude when I received my Bachelor of Arts in Leadership and Administration from Beulah Heights University. I was also inducted in the Beta Eta Beta Kappa Honor Society because of my academic achievements. I don't state these accomplishments to boast but to encourage someone who believes they can't succeed. I am a living witness that you can. If you don't believe in yourself or no one else believes in you, I will! When your circumstance tells you it will never happen, I'll encourage you that it can. I learned to speak inspiration, hope and encouragement over my own life when I didn't have others to encourage or lift me. I developed a tenacity to believe beyond what I saw because I understood it was only temporary. I've heard it said, *when giving birth to your dreams; don't let your contractions be your distraction.* Yes, it can be painful but it is part of the process. Don't allow discomfort that lasts for a short while destroy what is being birthed within you.

I understand that I've been empowered to empower others so I must continually increase my capacity to serve others. Conviction and passion have proven to be constant partners in my pursuit to grow. The power to rewrite your future is within you. Once you've been able to dispossess the layers that hindered your abilities to succeed, you'll experience a confidence that was always there but was hidden. You must be determined and make any and all essential adjustments to write a new destiny. Believe and move forward because it is within you. I know my purpose is to inspire hope, ignite passions and help rewrite futures. None of what I have experienced and achieved in my life could have been possible without faith. My faith in my God and most assuredly in myself drives me to stretch beyond where I am. I believe and I am well able to achieve my goals and aspirations. Please know I believe in you too.

I could not have succeeded in my transition to wholeness without the unwavering love, support and understanding of the love of my life, Curt Buckmire. My husband and gift from God for the past 24 years. I salute you, my love.

Blessing and grace be multiplied to you in your pursuit of the *real you.* I'm passing the mustard seed of hope and inspiration. I believe in YOU!

"There is no way I would enter the race without the assurance that God was in control."

Dan Moore, Sr.

Dan Moore, Sr. Founder/President APEX
African American Panoramic Experience Museum
135 Auburn Ave, Atlanta, GA 30303
Website: www.apexmuseum.org | Email: apexmuseum@aol.com |
Facebook: Apex Museum

APEX MUSEUM

President Dan Moore, Sr.
"How Firm a Foundation"

We are often asked about role models and who influenced our life. As I reflect on my life I can say unequivocally, my role model was my father. Of course I did not think so when I was growing up. Edwin Moore was a stern man who knew who he was. Even before it was popular he would sign official documents indicating his race as African. He talked about Marcus Garvey and the movement of that day with great pride.

It was my father that laid the foundation upon which I built my belief system and my life. I can truly say I have never admired anyone more. We were poor but we were rich. We were poor financially but rich morally and spiritually. And so with that foundation I was able to navigate life and accept what came my way. Changing the things I could and accepting the things I could not. But always walking with pride and dealing with honesty and integrity. Perfect, non-forgiven, yes. And so I credit my strong family as my foundation upon which I built my life. Being the youngest of ten children I knew hand me downs. I learned early how to love and respect my siblings - And without question, to respect my parents and elders. Life in Philly prepares you for life anywhere. I learned faith and trust at an early age even though I didn't know what it was or how to label it. I just knew as I walked my journey someone bigger than I was, is always in control.

The seeds that were planted in my life made the difference and hopefully the seeds I now plant will make a difference in the lives of others, many of which I will never know. I view planting seeds as an ongoing process that we do consciously and unconsciously. Whether those seeds are good or bad they fall on soil and often take root.

All of us have some purpose for being here. Sometimes we discover that purpose early, sometimes later, and sadly sometimes tragically. It has been and continues to be my purpose to be a vessel through which God can work. The question is sometimes asked, "Is the glass half full or half empty?" The question I always ask myself is, 'What is more important is what is in the glass?' Is the content hope or despair? Is it positive or negative? Is it healthy or unhealthy? This makes the analogy more important.

When you walk by faith, sharing and doing for others becomes natural. Often times it is not the big things but the small things that make the greatest difference and have the greatest impact. The parable of the sower told by Jesus talked about some seeds being eaten by the birds, some falling among the stones and not taking root but some falling on good ground and bringing forth fruit. And although one may plant and one may water it is God that gives the increase. That's why I feel compelled to pray as I give, that the seeds will fall upon good soil.
On this journey I have never feared doing what I felt inspired to do. Almost everything I have ever tackled from a carnal point it was doomed to failure. Starting companies with little capital, producing films with very little cash has been the norm for me. Not to suggest that we should not prepare a business plan. But I have always found it more assuring to have God at the center of any plan. It assures success.

I find to walk with God to be a great journey. His hands are big enough to hold me and the plan. His eyes see far enough to lead me where He wants me to go. His wisdom is deep enough to control the outcome. This is not to say it is always an easy road. I look at preparing myself, as running hurdles. When you clear one, there is another facing you. And this is repeated until you reach the finish line. There is no way I would enter the race without the assurance that God was in control. That's why I find it easy to multi task because, *The Lord is the strength of my life.* Psalm 27:1

And so as you sow your mustard seed, do not sow sparingly but bountifully. There is a harvest coming. Someday you will be able to look out over the field and see that harvest. A harvest waiting to be harvested.

"Why fit in when you were born to stand out!"

Twin of a Kind

TWIN OF A KIND FOUNDATION

Erin Green & Desiree Glover
"Stand Out!"

"Why fit in when you were born to stand out!" A motto that Erin and Desiree Glover stand by. These two beautiful and vivacious ladies are an example of uniqueness. They may look the same, have a similar walk, and carry themselves in the same manner but their personalities are quite unique. Erin is the observant of the two. She's known for examining first, take action second. Desiree is the bold and daring one, known to act first ask questions later. These contrasting personalities allows them to be there for each other, supporting and encouraging one other.

We didn't see things quite this way growing up. We tried our best to fit in with the in-crowd. Found it difficult to grab the attention of others and socially were labeled as 'awkward', ridiculed and bullied as youth for our lack of size and peculiar look. As children, growing up in school was rough. We were constantly criticized and ridiculed for our size and weight which was the butt of all jokes that we were unable to escape. Constant nagging and self-doubt was an unspoken voice that rang through our heads when we didn't believe in ourselves. Going after our dreams, taking new risks, and meeting new people was not an option for us. The negative things we told ourselves became routine and self-destructive.

Even though, nagging and the self-doubt of our child hood and adolescent past was a constant reminder that we would never succeed or go after our dreams, we were determined not to let our mindset be defeated. The Lord continued to place positive people in our lives to help us change our outlook and attitude on life and build our self-esteem. Through trials of negative self-doubt, the art of modeling was where we found our strength and confidence. We have always asked ourselves, "Why me, why us?" We're identical twins for a reason. It's a blessing from God. We have come to the conclusion that this blessing has a purpose. Our purpose is to share our testimonies with the world. It is meant for us to stand out and make a difference. So why fit in when we were born to stand out? It didn't take long for us to realize that the power of two had a greater impact than the power of one. From there, the journey began. It all began when a young lady told us, "You have their attention so what are you going to do with it?

The Lord continued to mold us into the image of what He wanted us to become by building our character to accept who we were and to love ourselves. More opportunities became available to us and what we believed was not within our reach became closer than we thought. Once we were able to replace our destructive thoughts with positive thoughts, our body image was no longer an issue and our size was used for a purpose. Taking risks helped us to overcome negative self-doubt. We found our confidence through a talent we discovered in our junior year of high school. Track-n-field gave us a foundation, a supportive family, and great memories. It also kept us busy and focused on other things rather than dwelling on the negativity. Our success as runners led us to receive scholarships to a college university.

Our defining moments that have led us out of the zone of isolation and fear was being able to conquer self-doubt and just simply take risks. We gained our confidence by appearing on Fear Factor (Twins Edition) in 2005; appearing on a music video by Slum Village titled, "Selfish" featuring Kanye West; while captivating our audiences on the runway with their dynamic synchronized strut, wearing the hottest trends and fashions of many fashion designers. Embracing size and appearance on countless amounts of print ads; obtaining over 30 years of combined experience in the mental health field; and most of all just being a twin and always knowing we have someone by our side.

The women we are today have a lot to do with the struggles of our past... FATHERLESS IN AMERICA, LIVING IN FEAR AND POOR CHOICES. This is our truths that kept us in bondage for so long, but has not broken us. We realized that what we have been through is our sole purpose of existence – to tell our story and pray that each individual that hears our story is blessed and is able to acknowledge their truth and begin their healing process. We stand before you with confidence, assurance, and faith that what the Lord has been continuing to instill in us is our TRUTH. But we didn't believe that to be true during our adolescent and young adult years. We have been fatherless all of our life. We feel that plays a HUGE part on our development and shaping of our minds. The decisions we have made in our past has a lot to do with the absentee of our father. We believe the absence of our father has taught us to make poor choices in life – relationships, parenting and love. Till this day our father does not know our struggle or how his absence has truly impacted our lives.

Oh, what we would give just to be heard, validated and normalized. An opportunity to experience how a man should love a woman and/or at least feel like no man is worthy of his 'little princesses'. The struggles we had to overcome to beat the odds and stop the recorder from those repetitive thoughts we told ourselves, such as: "Why our father and his family did not want us or want to be a part of our lives." "Are we not, what he wanted?", "Why doesn't he acknowledge us?", "Are we not important to him?", and "What did we do wrong?" are all thoughts that we continuously fed ourselves to a point of destruction, failure, rejection, abuse, and betrayal.

Fatherless daughters compared to those with present father figures are in higher risk of pregnancy and dropping out of school. Females without father figures often become desperate for male attention and have low self-esteem. Till this day our father does not know how him being absent in our lives truly made us feel or how it has impacted our lives. Being fatherless has prevented us from being freed from our own fears. We let fear, hurt, anger, disappointment and rejection consume us and become excuses as to why we accept anybody to fill the empty void that should have been filled by a man that was not ready to be a father.

When that opportunity came for us to confront our father, it was only the grace of God that allowed us to forgive and move forward from our past. We realized that his absence did not damage us, but through his absence it grew us closer to the Lord and gave us a purpose. HE taught us that we are loved and not alone; not to fear nor worry, that through HIM, HE strengthens and encourages us. We learned how to make bad decisions, before but that was only the first chapter in our book and that we have the opportunity to make better choices and rewrite the rest of our story. But if it weren't for the foundation of our faith we wouldn't have been able to forgive and would still be living in fear.

Our purpose is to share our testimonies with the world and make a difference.   To help youth and young adults reveal their story and accept it as their truth; take the truth and find purpose; love themselves for what they have endured and finally not live in fear to be able to tap into their potential and take risks in life. Erin Green and Desiree Glover are living testimonies of tapping into their potential and have formed the brand, Twin of a Kind (TOAK).

As motivational speakers, models, youth advocates, and founders of a non-profit organization, the twins are determined to be heard and seen. You can catch them on the runways in Los Angeles and New York or featured in magazines which will help to grab the attention they need to be heard. This will give TOAK a bigger platform to help the youth of today attack issues of self-esteem, bullying, abuse, sex, fear and relationships, to name a few. Excited to take their brand to the next level, the twins stated, "We are known for our motto, "Why fit in, when you are born to stand out," and after assessing what TOAK has to offer as a brand and product to the community and entertainment industry, it is evident that the world needs to know us and what we are doing to inspire, motivate and captivate audiences. We both realized that in order to pass our mustard seed and help others reach their potential in life; you can't be afraid to ask for help and tap into other peoples' gifts and talents. We asked and God answered through the help from others.

"Write the vision and make it plain on tablets."

Habakkuk 2:2 (KJV)

Author | Poet | Music Producer | Song Writer | Composer
Website: www.poetofpeace.com | Email: pop@poetofpeace.com |
Facebook: Poet of Peace | Twitter: poetofpeace | Instagram: poetofpeace | YouTube:
Poet of Peace

PLANTING SEEDS ENTERPRISE

Lawrence "POP" Rutherford
"Tag, You're It!"

My name is Lawrence Rutherford, but I go by the nickname P.O.P which stands for Poet of Peace. My purpose in life is to become a national, world-known, established author and evangelistic poet. I've already started to get my feet wet in these areas by publishing my first poetry and art book titled, Planting Seed for the Lost and Found. I have also established and produced my first CD, titled Lyrical Witness. My God given gifts and talents are changing lives all over the world, and it is a blessing to have people from all over the world reach out to me and let me know how they have been touched and blessed by what they have read and heard.

My main purpose in life is to be a world changer, by helping to make a difference and bring a change in people's lives through spoken word, music, and books. The power of faith had a major role that took part in my ministry, life, and business. Take for instance, I didn't know how I was going to be used by God to reach people, let alone make money doing something that I loved. That was the last thing that was on my mind. I remember it like it was yesterday on September 19, 1999, as I sat alone in my empty first apartment praying and saying to God that I didn't have any gifts or talents like singing, playing an instrument, or anything that I knew of to reach people and help them. Well...I am here to let you know that God heard my prayer and moved on my heart and had me grab a pen and write immediately.

These amazing words of poetry from heaven came to me instantly. Then I started memorizing them and having ideas of pictures and scriptures to go with it. It wasn't long after that, that churches, detention centers, nursing homes, and other places starting having me come speak and hear what I had to say. Several years later my ideas of pictures, poetry, scripture, and music all finally came together. The only problem was that I didn't know how I was going to get the funds for such an expensive project.

People kept telling me to do black and white photos so the cost would be cheaper, or just write poems without artwork. My answer remained- no, as I knew that was not how God wanted it. Then, I would have situations with artists not wanting to draw the artwork anymore or not wanting to draw them as I had envisioned for it to be, which left me having to find replacement artists. But, I persevered, I had unwavering faith, and I kept believing that the dream God had given me would have to come to pass, and it did.

I will admit that at one point my faith was deteriorating, and I sat for years not doing anything, until one day something sparked on the inside of me as I got a phone call from out of nowhere about my book. At that moment, all the pieces of the puzzle started coming together and people that God placed in my life started working with me to start the process of making my book project and my dream become a reality. Following my God given purpose lead me to come in contact with one person, who connected me with another person, who connected me to another until almost all aspects of my entire project had been completed.

Then God gave me an idea and showed me exactly how to support the cause of the book and CD. It was something I had worked on for twelve to fourteen years without giving up. Had it not been for the many sacrifices made, prayers prayed, financial and spiritual seeds sown in my life, and endurance to press forward despite of what things might have looked like, I surely would have failed. But even more importantly, God continued to be faithful to His promise and His word.

Jeremiah 29:11(KJV) reads, *"For I know the plans that I have for you, declares the Lord, plans to prosper you and not to harm you, plans to give you a hope and a future."* Galatians 6:9 (KJV) reads *"Lets us know to not get tired of doing what is good for at the right time we will reap a harvest if we do not give up."* With that said, if you have a dream and a vision that God has impregnated within you, then pray that He will birth it and bring it to pass. If you start it, then follow through and finish it. Never look at yourself as a failure if you run into a temporary road block. Get back up and try it again. Just because it seems as if there is no light at the end of the tunnel, trust and believe that with God, the light will always shine bright. You just have to keep walking, keep moving, and trust in God knowing that He has a plan for your life and He wants you to act on it. Move in faith knowing that He will make sure that the dreams and visions He has given you, will become reality.

In final, Habakkuk 2:2 (KJV) reads *"Write the vision and make it plain on tablets," (or paper in today's society).* The main reason I'm able to give advice and share my testimony is simply because I have been through the storm and down the valley and know what it is like to wonder how in the world, what you are wanting to happen so bad, going to happen. I will leave you with this, you just have to play T.A.G and know that you are IT! T-Think, A-Act, G-Go.

"People are often unreasonable, irrational, and self-centered. Forgive them anyway. If you are kind, people may accuse you of selfish, ulterior motives. Be kind anyway. If you are successful, you will win some unfaithful friends and some genuine enemies. Succeed anyway. If you are honest and sincere people may deceive you. Be honest and sincere anyway. What you spend years creating, others could destroy overnight. Create anyway. If you find serenity and happiness, some may be jealous. Be happy anyway. The good you do today, will often be forgotten. Do well anyway. Give the best you have, and it will never be enough. Give your best anyway. In the final analysis, it is between you and God. It was never between you and them anyway."

Mother Teresa

Women's Mentor | Author | Motivational Speaker | PR & Publishing Owner
Website: www.JavonaSmith.com | Email: admin@javonasmith.com | Facebook: JavonaS

PR & PUBLISHING CO.

Javona Smith
"The Seed"

As a result of molestation – my mother gave birth to me three months prematurely when she was only a child herself. No one should have experienced this, a thirteen year-old girl giving birth, especially when it was forced upon her. But she did the best, I believe, that she could do in her circumstance. However, I grew up needing a sense of identity from a solid, reliable source and I did not have that as a young girl. Sometimes husbands and boyfriends can do this at one level, but I think that most women long for a deeper source of affirmation – The affirmation of a father.

With my mothers' emotional detachment and eventual drug abuse, I grew up without both of my parents; my mother emotionally and my father physically. I developed issues that our society call, "daddy issues", and those issues sometimes revealed themselves inside my issues with God. Then my issues with God seeped into the rest of my life. Women who struggle with the absence of affirmation from their mothers or fathers can become very vulnerable and weak at certain points in their lives, especially when it comes to their belief about God. There is something about the love from a father that is very important for the development of self-esteem in a girl. With the abundance of single mother households and abusive or emotionally inattentive fathers, it should come as no surprise that there are droves of women who have an unhealthy need for attention from men. These women often grow into insecure, sexually aggressive, or promiscuous women who use men and then discard them. Similar to how their fathers did to them or their mothers.

I was no different; I experienced almost every symptom known to a motherless, or in my case, a parentless child: low-self-esteem, maladjustment, negative body image, sexual promiscuity, I even had sexual encounters with women because in my distorted perception – it was normal and acceptable. My mother did it; her friends in the hair industry did it, why not me? I learned that although I want to empower as many women as I can, being intimate with them sexually is not my cup of tea. When I made the decisions to live the life that I saw being lived, I didn't love myself. Eventually, I knew I had to remove all of the negative influences out of my life; even if one of the negative influences was my own mother. Looking back now, I don't even recognize that girl. But I will never forget her and how she helped me grow into the woman I am today.

The relationship I now have with my mother is extraordinary, we can talk about anything. But not like a mother and daughter, more like sisters. We have the most outrageous conversations and she is insanely funny! I love her deeply and I forgive her for everything. I understand that many of her unfavorable choices are largely due to her drug abuse. Getting to this point was very difficult, but the screaming, the tears, and the much needed conversations proved therapeutic for us. The experience of being her daughter has been the first step of learning how to love unconditionally. Loving her has taught me to love the person and not necessarily their behaviors or habits.

Like me, other motherless daughters tend to feel lost, out of place, and unsafe in the world. They may feel lonely and depressed, especially when at happy family gatherings with friends. Hating their body and wanting to alter it (with tattoos, piercings, breast augmentation, etc.) is not uncommon. Many of these women may have an urge to stay in the limelight. Not having the secure presence of a loving, supportive mother is detrimental to a girls' emotional development. But there is a bright side to being a motherless daughter. Women who grew up without a nurturing mother tend to be original thinkers, purpose-driven, empathetic, thoughtful, spontaneous, and resourceful.

Examples of women who grew up without mothers are: Marie Curie, Oprah Winfrey, Eleanor Roosevelt, Virginia Woolf, Marilyn Monroe, Princess Diana, Maya Angelou, Carol Burnett, Jane Fonda, Liza Minnelli, daughter of Judy Garland had a strained relationship with her mother while trying to care for her mother during her pill abuse and depression. Also, Madonna, and Rosie O'Donnell, emotionally abandoned women, like myself, are not included in this list because the world may not notice when this occurs.

If you can relate to having 'Daddy Issues,' or being a motherless child, identify that it is a possibility that the main issue of your problems lie in the fact that this is *your* emotional baggage. This awareness can be painful, because it brings up feelings of being unloved. If you are a woman, don't be afraid to bond with other women, or allow a man to get to know you before being sexually intimate with him. Doing so can help you heal. Learn to trust other women and recognize good men. See the strength and openness of other women and find comfort in being part of a sisterhood, something greater than just you.

Understanding the limitations of your parents may eliminate hurt and disappointment when they aren't playing their role effectively. Seek professional help if you are truly suffering. There are so many types of therapies out there, you could start a diary or journal, write a book, paint, sing, hire a counselor, life coach, or psychologist, or you can talk to your pastor, best friend, or complete stranger just to detox the emotional poison out of your system.

I overcame the turmoil of these difficult times by writing and reflecting on what was written once I revisit my journal. I remind myself that I am never really abandoned or unloved; for I have always been loved and appreciated by The Lord (Deuteronomy 31:8 KJV). I had come to realize that although I am the offspring of my parents, God is my manufacturer. So if I have any defects to fix, problems to resolve, or concerns to mull, I can always talk them over with Him.

It is now my understanding that my choices are solely my own. No one is to blame for what I have previously done or continue to choose to do. Every day is a chance to reinvent myself and grow into the woman I was created to be. Every day is an opportunity to take action to go where I envision my life going. I once heard someone say, "Action without vision is stumbling in the dark. And stumbling in the dark is poverty stricken poetry." Today, I choose not to live my life as poverty stricken poetry – I choose to live it abundantly, in spite of any and every choice I have made yesterday.

Some of us allow unkind, self-serving, irrational people and life occurrences to hinder us from becoming our best selves. Or we feel we have to balance who we love with what makes sense to do. There is a way to do both, if we allow ourselves to do them. We sometimes tell ourselves that we aren't good enough. But that is far from the truth. The truth is that you are more than good enough, you were created to win. You are a child of God and through Him all things are possible.

"In whatever you do, do it so well that no man living, no man dead, and no man yet to be born can do it any better"

Dr. Benjamin Elijah Mays

Founder & CEO of The V2L Corporation |
Executive Program Director of Alliance of Dreams, Inc. |
Brand Management | Business Development Consultant
Website: www.NickBartleypresents.com | Email: nick@V2Lcorporation.com |
LinkedIn: www.linkedin.com/in/nbartley | Facebook: V2Lceo | Twitter: V2Lceo

V2L CORPORATION

Nick Bartley, M.Ed.
"Evicted to Build"

I was born in the housing projects of Savannah, GA, to a single parent mother that raised 5 kids. I managed to always do well in school despite my shyness and extreme introverted demeanor. In any attempt to fit in, I downplayed my intellect to become an "average" student, as many other students do today. I later went to college, worked, obtained a master's, and started a business. I've always worked for everything that I needed because I never wanted to burden anyone. My take was to always work for everything, and ask ONLY when it was absolutely necessary, as this is still practiced to this day.

Growing up, I had been deemed an only-child, nerd, selfish, from an affluent upbringing, arrogant, etc... Needless to say, most of this was brought on by me. Even when I was young I was well-mannered, neat, took extreme care of myself and belongings, treated others with respect, and just simply carried an altruistic demeanor about myself and business in general. As I Matured, I realized that my journey was not only for me, but was also meant for someone else. It always amazed me that I may have to carry this load so others wouldn't have to. In the midst of my lowest moments, I wasn't allowed to die nor deemed to give up. I am a living example of what it means to not look like what you have been through.

My journey was never defined by how I looked on the outside although I was deteriorating on the inside. I spent three extra years in pursuit of a BS in Mathematics which was definitely not an easy task due to battling with depression. I confided in school counselors during this battle with a "spirit of depression" and somehow it seemed to have made things worse and led to an even deeper borderline suicidal mentality. Why? Because everyone thought they knew what a depressed person "looked" like. In those seven years, I had been robbed at gun point, experienced an apartment fire only to be moved and then burglarized, had a roommate that tried to take my life, was told that "I would never graduate with a math degree by a department "advisor", and experienced a series of health, mental, and financial issues that a person my age should not had had to deal with, but GOD knew how strong I really was, even when I was blinded by depression and hidden insecurities. After graduating with my math degree, things got worse before better.

Due to the suffrage of my G.P.A. finding a job was an entirely different journey despite the countless contacts in my direct network with recruiters, hiring managers, and other connect. There are some things that natural beings cannot help you out of. However, divine favor had a plan and I was given a temporary job as my bridge, but a shift in the atmosphere turned it into a professional career that many felt I was not qualified to do; therefore, I worked hard to show my work ethic. I lost my job shortly after not being able to deal with the pressures in one position later decreasing my salary by way of taking on another position because I pursued happiness and my passion.

I am well-known for motivating people to reach their fullest potential by challenging them in their thoughts to strive for better and to not think with such low aim. All my blessings have been a revolving cycle because as I receive, God always seems to place others in my life with a greater need and in obedience I gave as instructed.

When I first decided to start my blog (The168Life.tumblr.com) the intent was to document my journey as an entrepreneur, which would include the trials and tribulations that I endured. It is my hope that you gain insight from my personal experience that you may avoid the entrepreneurial hardships that I experienced.

After the approach of a 5 year milestone, the time had come for that chapter to close. But like any good book or dramatic episode, it didn't end pretty and the transition should have been the end of the line. Just as I told my students and the hundreds I was able to speak life into as they came to the campus, the words of Dr. Benjamin Elijah Mays kept resonating in my spirit… "In whatever you do, do it so well that no man living, no man dead, and no man yet to be born can do it any better." So I took one month as I was trying to get my affairs in order to seek the face of God and figure out what I did to deserve the outcome until I was reminded of "the" deal, which was that I was not to remain in my "temp" job past 5 year. I didn't factor in the fact that the temp job could become permanent with benefits and a salary close to $40k. Nonetheless, that assignment was done and while in the valley I created my company and petitioned for grad school for the fall (at the end of recruitment season for any program). In this instant the game had totally changed. I went from being jobless to entrepreneurship, I got accepted into my master's program, and I was selected as a featured contestant on a new game show that has reached international airwaves all within the first 6 months, finally, the eye of the tornado.

This transition tested every ounce of my faith and trust that God had a plan for my life as He revealed it would be used as an example to many that have dealt and/or dealing with what I have experienced. In the midst of nearly completing my 2 years of graduate work, my motivation for that field dwindled by more than 50% (still graduated with a 3.83 G.P.A.). My 2009 Altima, which I financed BRAND NEW, was repossessed because I didn't have the capital to make the payments forcing me to reacquaint myself with MARTA (Atlanta's public transportation). My living situation became unstable as I exchanged roommates, struggled to maintain all my bills with an uncertain cash flow which was frozen out of one home and landed into a condo where I remained until 7 months after the completion of my master's, only to end up on a sofa with my possessions in storage (which I still have). Last year I was blessed to regain independence with a new apartment and as the storm returned I was evicted only to be linked with a repurposed space that I called home.

The V2L Corporation will be known as the company that started from nothing and that carefully selected its clientele with the intent on delivering on its promise. I value everyone that gives me the opportunity to assist in making their vision a reality whether it's a logo, business card, website, and for some their actual business. My days of micromanagement ended April 23, 2009 and my best executed projects have been those where I wasn't looked at as a business owner just starting out.

After building a solid five year career foundation working at Morehouse College, I was led to pursue my long awaited entrepreneurial endeavor to own a conference and special events planning & design company. In 2009 that dream was realized with a trust fall on faith that led to the formation of V2L Events, LLC (now The V2L Corporation, LLC), an event planning & management firm focused on highlighting the client's brand image through their events. By 2011 the demand shifted to branding & marketing and fostered the development of the V2L Design Studio. The founding vision and current practice is to make V2L a "one-stop" branding solutions firm to assist with event planning, branding, and marketing in one seamless production package. Additionally, my commitment to assisting others in business and entrepreneurial development led to creating The Entrepreneurial Cooperative (2012) and The 168 Life Project (2014). These business endeavors has become a manifestation of what I had to learn to be my passion and ministry. My Testimony is the source of my inspiration and motivation to move forward. Not a rags to riches story, but one of how my life transformed into a pursuit to assist others in obtaining their life-long goals and ambitions. It is my prayer that my journey will not only help those who are reading, but also help you to pass on the mustard seed of faith that will sprinkles blessings into another individuals life.

I simply want to encourage you to **NEVER** give up on yourself. It doesn't matter how hard it looks, how rough times get, or how far it may seem that you have fallen, YOU will never be given a challenge in this life that you are unable to conquer. My business is my passion and labor of love that I genuinely care for and intercede in the business life of my clients. My credentials, experience, portfolio, and service delivery is my burden of proof of God's ability to give me success. (Note that your journey, whether as an entrepreneur or an employer, isn't defined by your role, but by how you execute it and your faith in God. Never allow others to define you or put you in a box. Know that no one is going to invest more into your vision that you are willing to put in.) I am blessed and humbled to have just celebrated the 5 year anniversary of my company V2L.

Evicted to Build: is a metaphor of how I had to not only die to myself, but had to be forced to separate from those people, places and things that were not needed for where I was destined to go. In that process comes the Building up of the new me which spreads the wealth by building up others. We are quick to try and hold on to things that do us more harm and have little desire to move out the comfort zone of complacency and content as a means to walk into our purpose. The more I prayed to God to allow me to follow HIS will for all that I was destined to do, the harder life seemed to get. The more I longed for material possessions, the more I began to lose, thereby making my hard work seem to be done in vain. But as I am reminded of the God I serve, the more I realize that my purpose and prosperity resided in my praise and thanksgiving for what I already have inside that needed to be shared with others. My faith grew stronger allowing me to better cope with living life on purpose and with purpose for the sake of saving someone else's. Now, I pass the mustard seed of faith onto you and your business endeavors.

"God is amazing, simply because He has chosen you to represent harvest in this season, to be a blessing on your journey to a purposeful destiny."

DeMarlo West

Founder & Owner Shadow Designs LLC | Celebrity Make Up Artist | Make Up Scientist Workshop Facilitator
Website: www.demarlowest.com | Email: info@shadowdesigns.org |
Facebook: DeMarlo West | Twitter: makeupscientist | Instagram: makeupscientist

SHADOW DESIGNS, LLC

DeMarlo West
"The Harvest"

DeMarlo West was born November 30, 1980 and raised in Milledgeville, Georgia to the proud parents of Larry and Eleanor West. DeMarlo attended the Baldwin County School System and received his diploma in 1999. Academically, he received his Bachelor of Arts degree in Sociology/Criminology from Paine College in Augusta, Georgia. After graduating from Paine, DeMarlo attended Troy State University in Troy, Alabama and received his Master's degree in Education with a concentration in Counseling/Psychology.

DeMarlo's childhood was simply amazing. He constantly honors his parents for the remarkable job they did in raising him. DeMarlo has two sisters Takisha Thompson and Summer West. His family structure afforded him with the knowledge of being able to practice biblical principles while developing a personal relationship with God.

DeMarlo comes from a strong musically talented family that enforced spirituality and Christianity as a daily practice. While growing up in the church, DeMarlo knew the importance of having and maintaining a personal relationship with God, understanding his Word, and learning how to practice faith. His parents consistently made God relevant in the home and taught him that all things are given as a blessing from the Almighty God. During his college years, DeMarlo was a musician for several churches, singing and playing the piano and/or organ. Throughout his life, DeMarlo ensured that God is at the forefront of everything he does.

West is to owner and founder of Shadow Designs LLC, a freelance makeup artistry. He began his journey of enhancing natural beauty in 2004. His motivation and mission was to ensure that clients not only look beautiful, but also feel and understand the essence of beauty captured within them. He is well known for conducting "Tour of Tutorials" throughout the USA and abroad. His tutorials have equipped clients with the skill set to execute soft editorial looks, to evening glam.

DeMarlo has five (5) apprentices under his tutelage, coaching and inspiring makeup artists to achieve their maximum potential. DeMarlo has worked with celebrity clients such as Donald Lawrence & Company, Jonathan Nelson, Blanche McAllister Dykes, VaShawn Mitchell, Pastor Paula White, LaShun Pace, The Anointed Pace Sisters, LaTrice Pace, Monica Lisa Stevenson, Lacretia Campbell, and many others.

West first experience with makeup and cosmetics was when his cousin Jon Peeler a former makeup artist, introduced it to him. Peeler unexpectedly asked West to take him to a wedding that he had to do makeup for. West was very uninterested however he agreed to attend anyway. While sitting there observing Peeler transform this client, it sparked a sense of creativity in West. Most of all, he was able to see how the client's confidence changed within a matter of minutes. It was at that moment, West knew that makeup is not only about application, but more so a ministry. After practicing on his youngest sister Summer, he started with arching eyebrows and learning the structure of brows. Then he began to experiment with eye shadows and trying to figure out how it works. His parents observed that their son had another talent that was unheard or spoken of and they encouraged him to keep practicing until he perfected it. A few months passed and West visited a mall with a friend that encouraged him to apply for a position at the MAC counter. He was extremely intimated and frighten because all the other employees were professionals and he was a baby in the makeup world. To his surprise, the manager offered him the opportunity to interview and demonstrate a complete makeover in front of the store. You can only imagine how nervous it was to pull this off. After his makeup demonstration, the manager offered West the job. This is a true testament of knowing that God has crafted your journey and aligning you to travel to your destiny. West watched every employee strategically to learn different techniques to execute looks for his clients. After about four months, West gained a clientele that afforded him the opportunity to leave MAC and do freelance makeup. West relied on the teachings of his parents and the promises of God when he made the leap of faith to go freelance. He asked God to teach him the way, create other lens of creativity so that his craft can become better. Since 2005, West has been a freelance makeup artist and has not worked any cosmetic counter since that time.

Because of his creative nature, West began to ponder opening his own makeup company. He began to ask God, "what should I name it and what would be the purpose?" God began to reveal to West what his purpose was in the cosmetic industry. It was not to be limited to being a makeup artist, but to touch lives by enhancing the appearances of people. When people know they look good, they began to feel good, and lastly they began to treat others good. It lights a sense of self confidence and lift self-esteem. West professional background includes but not limited to substance abuse counseling and group therapy. That experience equipped him with the tenacity to handle emotional situations that sometimes can be life threating. So the skills that he used in his professional environments prior to makeup, he made those same skills transferable to the makeup world.

DeMarlo has been a brother, husband, counselor, minister, best friend, and much more to clients that has an experience with him. But DeMarlo's consistent message to his clients is, God is the author and finisher of our faith. Therefore, he crafts supernatural purposes for us to naturally fulfill. When we live in purpose, it opens the avenue for God to build and tear down whatever is not conducive for the journey. Activating your faith is knowing that you are believing God for the things that we seem to think are impossible. You are in fact standing on promises that you cannot see and unaware how it will manifest. Trusting and believing in God is a plea that you solely rely on his guidance, direction, and instruction. When you operate in ministry throughout your daily lives, God equips you with the words to say, things to do, and prayers to pray. Living this kind of life, fertilizes what he has in store just for you.

God's word are promises for your entire life. Whatever it is that you want to achieve, it starts with the belief that it will happen. Understanding that God writes your destiny and inserts the ability for you to live beyond measure as it is His will for your life. The greatest leader and achiever is one that has the intelligence of teaching others how to be better than them. Therefore, passing the mustard seed is in fact a practice of fertilizing purpose to become a harvest in someone else's life. In that harvest, others are blessed with the needs of that time and tools to handle times that are to come. God is amazing, simply because He has chosen you to represent harvest in this season, to be a blessing on your journey to a purposeful destiny.

[2] And be not conformed to this world: but be ye transformed by the renewing of your mind, that ye may prove what is that good, acceptable, and perfect, will of God.

Romans 12:2 (KJV)

Author | Leadership Consultant | Workshop Trainer | Public Speaker
Website: www.remeteka.com | Email: ReMeTeka@gmail.com |
Facebook: TekaDowner | Twitter: ReMeTeka

RE-ME: REINVENT ME

Teka Allen
"Faith Renewed"

The truth is, I have never been that good at explaining me or my services to others. However, I have recently uncovered a new truth as it comes to sharing my storms and trials with others, those catastrophic events almost roll off of my tongue as easy as it is to say hello to a perfect stranger in the South! I am learning that there is power in our testimony as the word declares we overcome by the blood of the lamb and the word of our testimony. So, in an essence the more I share, the more liberated I become.

In 2013, I endured the storm of a lifetime and I never even saw it coming. There were days I fought just to get out of bed to get my son to school then right back in bed because life was hurting so bad. I was battling depression and wasn't even sure if I fully believed depression existed or not. I also battled with myself, there were two real forces that I became aware of that were a real part of me, my flesh and my spirit. My flesh and my spirit were in a daily tug of war for my life and I felt it. One would show me my current circumstances, my failures, my heartache, and command that I give up. The other would show me God's promises, God's provisions, God's love and command that I stay in the fight. Prior to 2013, I was pretty content with my life, I was content with my working environment, my personal life, and even my decision to leave my job and pursue full-time entrepreneurism which would include a big portion of building church staff, so, that meant I would technically be doing ministry full-time. So, of course I thought I was fully on God's side since I was opting to do "His" work. I even named my company His Consultants, so I just knew it would be blessed and business was going to be amazing! The exact opposite happened. My clients weren't coming in as I anticipated, but my bills were still faithfully showing up like clockwork. My closest relationship ended suddenly and my huge circle of support vanished. Life as I knew it came crashing down and I had no explanation for it. I cried out to God begging that He see how I was faithful unto Him. I cried that He would see how I was in Church Sunday after Sunday ministering to His people. I begged that He would remember my Thursday's that I gave for His service, My Wednesday's for His youth, I pleaded with Him to remove the devils access to my life and my finances and mend my heart. I told Him I walked away from a good paying profession to do His work and His people were ignoring my services. I pleaded that He be mindful of my service…then He spoke! After all my many days of crying out, fussing, and pleading with God, He finally spoke. And it was a simple "I've missed you daughter."

See what I didn't realize was during all of this which I thought was killing me was actually restoring my communication with the Father. The pain caused me to cry out to Him constantly, it caused me to seek after Him. I would wake up crying out to Him and I would fall asleep crying out to Him. To hear Him say "I've missed you," broke my heart. That was a breaking that still brings tears to my eyes as I recall those words. I realized that I was doing all of the work of Ministry, but I was missing the relationship with The Father. I was gaining the world, but literally losing my soul which honestly profited me nothing. This storm that had forced itself into my life was beginning to look purposeful. I can't lie to you and tell you that it got easier that day, because it didn't, but I was beginning to see a glimmer of light in the midst of so much darkness. Then, the Lord tasked me with empowering His people through a movement known as Re-Me, which is short for Reinvent Me. Can I be honest with you for a moment? I did not want to encourage myself let alone other people! As I told you earlier I was just introduced to the storm of a lifetime and now God is tasking me with a movement of encouragement and empowerment for His people in the midst of the storm…WHAT?! I got angry, sad, and scared all at the same time. I thought how can I encourage another when all hell is breaking out in my life, how can I encourage others when I can't find encouragement for myself? But somehow I knew I had to do it, I knew I had to push the Ministry of Reinvention to others. I had to push through my feelings, my circumstance, and honor the work that was being requested of me. I had to rely on that mustard seed size faith that was already on the inside of me. It was extremely tiny, barely existed, but it was my job to water it with The Word of God. I had to cultivate that seed with the supplies that He had already given me. It took me taking my eyes off of the storm and looking at what was already around me. In that time I realized, it may not be all good, but it most certainly isn't bad either! I understood in the midst of this storm that I was carrying a seed that had to grow and God had already given me mid-wives to help me deliver my seed of purpose.

You see, I thought I had lost the best relationships, but He was showing me those relationships weren't qualified to help bring forth my seed during that season. I thought I was losing my mind, but I had to in order to gain the mind of Christ. I literally had to lose it all to gain everything, I became a living epistle of the message Re-Me. So my friend, the mere fact that you are reading this, I pray that you find encouragement in some way. I pray that you realize it may be hard reaching your goals and purpose, it may even seem impossible, but if God has tasked you with such an assignment He has equipped you as well. We have all been giving a measure of faith, reach down and find yours. Work your faith and grow it. Never ever forget, without faith it is impossible to please God. So it may seem crazy to others, but know that your Father is pleased by your believing in what you can't see. Be blessed and don't forget to pass the mustard seed!

"ME AGAIN"

So, when does the new chapter of my life begin? Today looks and feels just like yesterday. I do see a tad bit of hope veering at me in the corner, but she stands so far off that I have resolved to ignore her presence for the time being. I swear this night mare repeats every day and I just can't seem to find the dang button that restarts my life anywhere! I have been fortunate enough to click this button on my computer, phone, and even my handy dandy electronic notebook. But nowhere in my life have I identified that button which with one click everything stops, goes blank, and starts anew. How frustrating it is dealing with the same issues day in and day out, the same bill collectors' day in and day out. I know this may come as a surprise to you Mr. Bill collector person, but if I didn't have your money yesterday, it's a pretty good chance I won't have it today! Day in and day out this same chapter keeps repeating itself…until today.

Today feels different. Today I feel like I have the strength to gather all the things I cannot control and escort them to an unknown exit of my life. I feel like I can begin again or rather be me again. Today I am embarking upon a new strength all on my own. I didn't have to call mama pleading for prayer, or my girlfriend asking for guidance, while simultaneously texting my pastor, 'please pray for me.' I just simply feel like fighting to become me all over again. Today I realized that I have been in a dark place for far too long. My days were stolen by an unseen enemy who didn't play fairly and now I am ready to call him on his foul play.

Today I realized that darkness was residing in my home without helping with the mortgage whatsoever. Today I realized there is power in becoming me. I finally found the remedy for me or my internal restart button. That button has reinvention all on it, as a matter of fact, I have nick named it Re-Me! Well, today I pressed it on the day my house foreclosed. (*"Me Again", an excerpt from my Re-Me blog*)

I encourage you to press the Re-Me button and pass the mustard seed.

"I've learned that people will forget what you said, people will forget what you did, but people will never forget how you made them feel."

Maya Angelou

THE HAVEN LEARNING CENTER

Denise Braswell
"Seek Him"

End with realizing the importance of touching the lives of the children as well as their families, everyone I come in contact with is my ministry.

Let me begin by stating, my faith in God is the foundation of who I am and the purpose of what I do. I believe God put me on this earth for a purpose. I further believe that I have the ability to choose whether to use my life for His purpose and plan or to use my life for my own selfish reasons and goals. I have chosen the first. It is my goal to use each day to glorify His Name and to affectively be a witness for His kingdom. With this said, I make every attempt to conduct by day to day business practices, personal relationships, and ministry endeavors in the very same manner.

In my professional life I own and operate an academic learning center. It is my duty to teach students how to become the best possible students. I provide my students with the educational tools necessary for their academic success. Although I didn't realize it but this business was birthed many years ago. I would speak about doing this type of work many years prior to its existence. I would work with students in my own home for free in order to help them achieve their academic goals.

My personal life has been filled like turmoil like many others people. My marriage has suffered for many years. My husband and I have spent many years arguing and toying with idea of divorce. For several years we only stayed together because we had two children and a thriving church; so we make attempts to work things out. Believing that God bought us together, even when we weren't getting along takes faith. Holding on to the fact that God is able to turn things around was the hard part. We have been married now for almost 25 years and we spent 20 years fighting, disagreeing and angry with each other. It has been a difficult journey but the one thing my husband and I have always agreed on is our belief in God and His plan for our life.

My purpose in life is to share the gospel, although I don't preach, I believe that my life is a witness and my faith holds it all together. Without faith the bible says that it's impossible to please God. I have applied my faith in seeking guidance for all areas of my life. I have asked God for instruction in my marriage. I have asked God for direction in running my business. God has provided in all of these areas.

My story of starting a business from ground up with no mentor, no investors and business plan while working on what seemed like an impossible marriage. When you feel like giving up just listen to the still voice of the Lord. And listen to what he said. He simply told me to hold on. To hold on to the man who was born to be my husband and hold on to the business which he had birth in me. At the time neither of them seemed to be working. I would often feel lost, alone and incapable to run a business. But when I would seek the Lord, He would speak to my heart. He would provide me with the confidence to know Him and to follow his instruction to become a better business owner and wife. God would literally speak to me about how to communicate with my husband. He would speak to me about what tasks to carry out for the business. I can honestly say that I feel strange suggesting that I own a business for the truth is that this business is His. Everything that it accomplishes should give Him glory because He did it all. My role was simply to carry out the instructions given to me.

Faith with a persevering attitude has allowed me great success. Life can bring hardships and difficult times but knowing how God loves me and has blessed me, for me He has made what I had considered to be trails now seem more like lessons in trust. I have learned to trust God and to take Him at His word. When my marriage seemed unable to work, God said differently. When the business was functioning at a hand to mouth level, God said don't worry. It was not until I believed what God was saying more than what I was seeing did I understand the necessity of faith. I now appreciate ever trial, situation, and uncomfortable circumstance as part of my education in learning to trust Him more and more each day. I have learned to hold on to God and not focus on what any situation might seem like.

If I could provide any advice to anyone it would be, to do anything it takes to establish a relationship with God and become determined in that which you're are called to do. Your calling doesn't have to be preaching in the formal sense. Your calling could be to help people in need, to teach students, to encourage, to raise your children, and care for your home. Whatever you feel God has planned for you do that, with a never give up attitude.

My calling to education and to encouragement is not new or even original however it is my calling. I have come to know that it is what I have been born for. It is what I do each day and I will continue to do it regardless of an attached income or not. It's not about the money, it's about the mission of introducing people to The Lord God.

My issues might be different from others, but what can be gained from my story is that God loves us all the same and what He has done for me, He is surely willing and able to do for all. He wants us to come to Him. He wants us to seek Him for guidance. He wants us to believe in Him. If we do set our mind that giving up is not an option, we would hang around long enough to see success. Too often we give up on our marriages and opt for divorce rather than putting forth more effort in becoming a better spouse. Most of the time when things are not working, we are the one's which require the most change and most work. I was able to come to grips with my contribution to a bad marriage and began the long road to change. My husband and I are now better for it and the business is thriving.

*"Now faith is the substance of things hoped for,
the evidence of things not seen."*

Hebrews 11:1 (KJV)

Co-Owner of E3TV | Independent Film Writer | Director | Producer
Website: www.fn2sproductions.com | Email: fntwos@gmail.com |
Facebook: Altuawn Nelson | Twitter: @altuawn1 | Instagram: altuawn_nelson

FROM NOTHING TO SOMETHING PRODUCTIONS

Altuawn Nelson
"During Difficult Times"

Being born in a lower socioeconomic environment caused me to feel hopeless from the start. As I grew older, I lost a lot of my peers to crime or prison due to a lack of patience. Most of them wanted money quickly so waiting wasn't an option. They sold drugs, car jacked, boosted clothes, robbed or did whatever else to fight the terrible feeling of not having anything. To add to my stress, my mother fought alcoholism daily, so she'd drink and speak about her issues or curse everyone out in her presence. Needless to say, her habit caused me to go to school many days on a few hours of sleep. To escape the frustration, I spent some nights in the trap house; this was the house where the drug dealers sold drugs. They welcomed me as a little brother or a son and always wanted me to do the right thing. Through the nights, I never thought about the consequences of going to jail if the police kicked in the door. I just enjoyed the peace and all of the stories they shared about life.

There wasn't a day that passed that I didn't see a way out of that place. If I could've ran away and lived with a family that was wealthy, I would've. Food Stamps and Section 8 were our means of survival. There was always a limitation on how much food we could eat at a time and things got tough towards the end of the month, as food ran low while we awaited the food stamps for the following month to come. Mama didn't pay the gas bill again this month, so it's back to using the electric heater to get through these cold winter nights, along with going to relative houses to take baths and eating a lot of microwavable foods. Get me out of this madness please. I'm seeing my partners hit these licks for rims, they're riding clean, and staying with money, but I know it's not right to take someone's possessions. I wouldn't want anyone to take anything from me, so I'm going to stay away from that. I've applied for jobs, but no one has called me back. Lord am I doing something wrong. Why me? It seems as though I'm left broke in a struggling household to only hear stories and witness people harming one another all for money and status. What's the purpose? It's like I'm living two different lives. School is cool but you didn't design me to hang out with the nerds, I'm always around the thugs. The guys that my mama informed me to be careful around, but

I'm lost because you won't allow me to do the things that they do. Even if I tried, they wouldn't let me. Something deep down is telling me that I'll make it out of this place as long as I keep my faith and stay on my grind, which is a broke one.

In 2006, I finally escaped the neighborhood and went off to college. Even there, I was more interested in studying behavior patterns and listening to stories. Needless to say, I stood out there as well. The feeling of being stuck in the middle again visited me. While everyone else was having a good time, I was dealing with grown people's issues. The mother of my kids conceived my first child when I was 20 years old, so instead of enjoying myself, I was working to take care of my seed. Needless to say mama still needed help in the hood, so I was paying some of her bills and mine too trying to stretch $10.00 per hour. Lord why me? I thought escaping the hood was the answer. I'm faced with the same situation again. I'm struggling and still feel as though I have no place in society. Why can't I do what the others are doing and when I try, why isn't it fulfilling? What's the purpose? One day a voice in my head said," get a pen and a pad and start writing", so I took heed. What I started to form were narratives that I heard in the hood while hanging around.

All of the stories I heard started to make sense now. That young lady who everyone else slept with and threw away that opened up to me about why she slept around. My mother sharing her inner thoughts about life. Those robberies gone badly. The stories about how the drug dealers would do the right thing if they could do it all over again but they felt they were in too deep. That college student that played around and fell so far behind that they didn't feel the need to continue. They all made sense now. These things were shared with me to deter others from taking the same routes they chose. Not only did they share their inner thoughts, but they all informed me about what they would've done differently if they could redo life. If God would've given me what I wanted as a child, a youth, or a college student, maybe I wouldn't have been so opened and paid attention to the stories of others to actually write about them.

Throughout life I've always had to have faith that I'd gain an understanding of why God was putting me in those situations and why I was more different than others. Life is based on choices. With choices comes rewards or consequences. I could've easily picked up and gun and robbed someone or bought some crack and sold it. That was quick gratification, but I chose to hold on to my faith that everything was going to be okay. I've grown to realize that I was different because I was designed to lead others and display the good in them. A lot of times, we want to run away from our obstacles and back to comfort, which isn't a wise move. If we have faith and learn what needs to be learnt during that trial, on the other side lies the blessing. If the sun shined every day, we wouldn't exist as humans. We may not like rainy days but they play a large role in the maintenance of the eco system as well; hard times and struggles take place to develop strength.

Embracing my tribulations and believing that one day I'd figure out my purpose has led to me producing a documentary that we're touring called "The Alto Adjustment", writing short and feature films, and becoming part owner of a network that airs on Google TV and Roku called "E3 TV". If those adversities didn't occur, I wouldn't have any stories to write. Again, I challenge you all to accept the hard times and learn from them. You never know what God has in store. The blessings awaits you!

"Faith without works is dead."

James 2:26 (KJV)

Glamorous Events, LLC Founder | Author | Event Planning & Consulting Firm Website: www.theglamqueen.com | Facebook: theglamconsultants | Twitter: @glameventsceo | Instagram: jess_speaks_life

THE GLAM CONSULTANTS

Jessica Anderson
"Faith is Not Dead"

In 2014, I can honestly look back over my life and say, "I am so glad that I kept the faith and made it through." Today, I have so many titles that I am able to put behind my name that I am grateful for: Mother, Entrepreneur, Speaker, Author, Life Strategist, Mentor… this list can go on and on. It wasn't always this way. I wasn't always excited about who I was. But God. I made it through the detours of life because of my faith and trust in God.

There was always a stigma that women who ended up in an abusive relationship came from a single family home or grew up in that type of environment. It was often said that people that become homeless have no family or support system. What if I told you that neither of those claims are true? As the youngest daughter of the typical two-parent, middle class home in the nineties; I grew up dreaming of sweet success and happy endings. Upon graduating high school, all of those dreams seemed to be coming true. I had not a care in the world. I had been accepted into a few different colleges and after much deliberation, settled on a small HBCU in the middle Georgia area. I was ready for the next stage of my life to begin, or so I thought.

At 19 years old, I found myself physically abused, homeless, a functioning alcoholic and to make my storm worse, I found out that I was 2 ½ months pregnant. How could I have faith in such turmoil? How could I see past all of the negativity that was happening in my life? Martin Luther King, Jr. said, "Faith is taking the first step even when you don't see the whole staircase". That's it! I had to take the first step. No matter how small or big, making the first step is what matters. I had to remember that even in the times that I left God, He was still right there for me and with me. He never gave up on me. There were times while I was in my storm that my fears exceeded my faith. You have to know and understand that fear and faith cannot exist at the same time. Often times, we focus so much of our energy trying to reduce our fears that we lose our faith. You can't focus on the size of your fears; you have to focus on the size of your faith. What you focus on will grow! Theologian, John Piper, once said, "Fear is a hollow darkness in the future that reaches back through time to rob our joy now by belittling the sovereign goodness of God. But if we are in Christ, if we cling to him by faith, we don't have to be afraid." Fear ends when your faith begins.

"Now faith is the substance of things hoped for, the evidence of things not seen." (KJV)

I hoped for a better day, I hoped for a better tomorrow and by faith, I received. It was not easy and everyday was not full of sunshine. It was a journey that I truly learned my dependency on God. True faith is trusting God even when it doesn't make sense. You have to get to a place that having faith and trusting God's divine plan will work for your good is all that you have to get you through that moment. I used my pain for my purpose to increase the Kingdom. Every day, I had to say, "Yes, God! Even though it's hard and I can't see my way, I will continue to walk by faith and not by sight. I trust you!"

Walking by faith is an everyday journey. It's a lifestyle that you have to work towards each day. Faith is living with certain boldness, confidence and with expectancy that everything will work out, because it will. If ever I find myself losing faith, I start to not only remember where God has brought me from, but I also think about a blind person. As random as that may seem, just think about it. A blind person's entire existence is living by faith because they cannot see what is immediately in front of them, but they always take a step. They have faith that the path that they are traveling is clear and even in the times when they stumble; they have people around them who will help lead them in the right direction. Surround yourself around people who will encourage you in your faith, write down affirmations to read each morning before you start your day to remind you to keep the faith, take at least 10 minutes each day to get quiet and listen for God to speak to you. My favorite quote in the bible comes from James 2:26, "Faith without works is dead."(KJV). God can and will do great things in your life, but you have to do your part, as well.

Eleven years after my storm, by faith, I made it! I got my degree; I started my own business and started mentoring young ladies through dancing. I am living my life every day, by faith. Storms still come up in my life, but by faith, it always works out for my good.

"And those he predestined, he also called; those he called, he also justified; those he justified, he also glorified."

Romans 8:30 (NIV)

DOROTHY "PENNY" JONES

Dorothy "Penny" Jones
"I AM"

Dorothy was not exactly what would be considered the "coolest" name for a teenager. I wasn't the most popular girl in high school, quiet and easily intimidated. Because I was bullied about my name since elementary school, I took matters into my own hands and requested that everyone call me either 'Dee" or 'DJ' (Penney to family). Looking back, I believe this is where my identity issues began. My self-esteem was rather low and I had no idea who I really was. Dorothy? Dee? DJ? PK (preacher's kid). I was trying to figure it all out. Being a preacher's kid, I couldn't do a lot of the things the other kids could do. I couldn't go to the parties or hang out after the games. But, I finally found something that was as natural to me as breathing. Running. I loved running track, and it was the only activity that I participated in after school, and I was good at it. So good that I was receiving college offers my sophomore year. My future was looking pretty good for a 15 year old. Then everything changed.

In August 2004, I went to the hospital for surgery on my right inguinal hernia. As I sat in the operating room, gown on, IV in place, the nurse came in and uttered those words that would forever ring in my memory. Those words that sent my mind into an immediate frenzy. "Ms. Jones, we can't do the surgery.....you're pregnant." My mom and I looked at each other in utter disbelief. This couldn't be true. I had broken up with my boyfriend six months prior and decided that I was going to stop missing track practice to have sex and focus on my schoolwork. I slowly accepted the fact that this was my reality and in four short months I would meet him or her. My mind was bombarded with all types of questions. What about school? What about those scholarships? What about college? What are people at school going to say? What are people at the church going to say? I was devastated by this news, and I cried for days walking around with my head down in shame. My irresponsible actions not only affected my life but my parents' lives as well, not to mention this little person growing on the inside of me. How can I parent this child when I'm still a child myself? I didn't have all the answers but nonetheless, in December 2004 this 8lb 13oz child became my reality and changed my life forever. Using my son as my motivation, I graduated from high school, earned athletic and academic scholarships and in 2000, I've graduated from college with a BBA. All Glory to God!

I had thoughts of becoming a motivational speaker to young teenage mothers. I wanted to encourage them to stay in school and stay focused. They needed to know that there was so much more to life in spite of having a child and being an unwed, teenage mother. Unfortunately, that thought remained a thought. I allowed fear and doubt to creep in and I talked myself out of fulfilling a passionate dream to save others from making the same mistakes I had made. Even though I overcame the statistics that doomed teenage mothers to becoming high school dropouts, I found myself falling prey to another statistic.

By the age of 30, I had been married and divorced twice. I questioned myself, wondering if my marriages failed because of me. Did I demand too much? Did I not give enough? Am I not enough? As an adult, I found myself dealing with some of those same insecurities I did as a teenager. In my first marriage I was very strong willed, stubborn, mean, and selfish; none of which I recognized during the marriage. During my second marriage I was adamant not to repeat the same mistakes. I resolved within myself that I had changed, and things would be different this time. I was back in church consistently, and involved with the dance ministry. My pregnancy, although a bit challenging, was a good thing. Unlike the first time, I was older and married and everyone celebrated and anticipated the arrival of our little baby boy. I wasn't ashamed of my swollen belly; I could rub it proudly with the hand that displayed my wedding ring. I was happy. This time I was the exact opposite. I wasn't mean or strong willed. I was still stubborn and selfish but nothing like whom I was in the first marriage. Or maybe I was. At some point I felt as though I lost myself. I was too passive to communicate my needs to my husband. I became very withdrawn from everyone, even from my family. For a short period of time I was under no spiritual leadership. I was lost. I was alone. It didn't last, and I found myself divorced again, two children, single, and unfulfilled. What is happening to me? I am a good mother. I have persevered through some trying times. I've successfully completed high school and earned my bachelor's and master's degree. So why am I so unhappy?

Time went on. I started a new job so I would be able to provide for my boys. So now, I'm feeling independent and strong. Things are looking up. I can't go to church because of my work schedule but HE understands because I have to work to feed my children, right? About two years later my boys and I moved to our first house. It was a rental but it was perfect for us. I was back in the church, singing on the praise and worship team, and leading the dance ministry. I'm definitely heading in the right direction. One would think. It was January 2008, and I wasn't feeling too well. No need to go to the doctor, I recognized this feeling. I was pregnant! Pregnant out of wedlock, again? Immediately I reverted back to that 16 year old girl. Full of shame and disappointment. This time it's worst. I'm not a child that just made a mistake. I'm a grown woman. I know better. I'm not being made to go to church at this point. I'm going because I understand that's where I need to be. I'm on the praise and worship team. I'm opening myself to everyone in the sanctuary and poisoning them with my sinful indiscretions. I'm overseeing young ladies, talking to them about keeping themselves and loving themselves and validating themselves so that they won't look to others for it. All lessons that I sadly realized…..I still hadn't learned myself. I have to make this right. I'm having a girl this time. I need to be an example to her of what it means to be a strong, Christian woman. So I married her father and attempted this marriage thing again. Weakly built on an unstable foundation, it too fell apart.

Three times divorced, three children, I give up! Thoughts of suicide danced in my head. Scenarios of driving down the road full speed ahead toward a big truck. My children will be well taken care of and I won't keep messing up their lives. What has this done to my eldest, who remembers the stepfathers and the many attitudes and personalities of mommy? What have I taught him about stability and marriage? What can I teach my daughter? I was broken! "Ok God, I quit. I surrender all." It was at this point that I truly began to seek the face of God and ask Him, "Who am I? Before I started thinking that I knew, better than you, what was best for me, who did you call me to be?" I wanted to be whole, in my mind, in my body, in my emotions, and in my spirit. Not just for me, but for my children; Jovan, Kaden and Alaina. I wanted everything God had for me. I grew tired of trying to do things according to my will and by my power. After a lot of praying, consecrating, wailing and warring, God began to show me my purpose and destiny. I questioned, "How am I going to do that? I'm not skilled enough. I don't have the training. I don't have the confidence." He gave me Romans 8:30, moreover, whom He did predestinate, them He also called: and whom He called, them He also justified: and whom He justified, them He also glorified."

I've heard about faith, I've learned about faith, I've seen others operate in faith, but it wasn't until after that encounter that I can say I've totally and truly walked in it. I went from being on a job for 5 years, married and living in a beautiful house to being laid off, divorced and under foreclosure. It has been my faith that has kept me smiling. It has been my faith that keeps me worshipping and praising. It is my faith that keeps me in the presence of God. I know now who I am and most importantly whose I am. I believe that He is indeed my source, my keeper, my sustainer, and my provider. My faith keeps me from worry. My faith keeps me from depression. My faith keeps me from feeling defeated. My faith reminds me of Romans 8:30. I'm predestined. I'm called. I'm justified. I was broken, but my faith makes me whole. I had low self-esteem, but my faith reminds me that I am the righteousness of God. I was unsure of who I was, metamorphosing into who I thought others wanted me to be. But it is my faith that causes me to walk confidently in who my Creator created me to be for Him.

I believe I went through those struggles to encourage others, both male and female. Seek the presence of God, know your purpose and destiny and then have faith to walk it out. It won't always feel good. It won't always look like what you think it should look like. You may lose some friends and loved ones but with God, all things are possible. Trust and believe that, God will take care of you better than you can take care of yourself. He knows your end from your beginning. Walk blindly by faith in the fear and admonition of the Lord. That's how I made it through. That's how I'm making it through.

I'm not that depressed, low self-esteem having, suicidal thought provoking person I was in the past. She was a result of NO FAITH. She was a result of trying to do things in her own power. She was a result of being broken and looking to man, and her husbands, to fix her. She was a result of hiding her pain to appear to be someone she didn't know she was. But she, now, is dead. I am whole! I am whole in my mind, I am whole in my body, and I am whole in my spirit. I am predestined. I am called. I am justified. I am the righteousness of God. I am a worshipper. I am a successful entrepreneur. Dorothy, in Greek, meaning 'Gift of

God'. That's who I am. I am a gift of God. I may not know the final outcome of my purpose and destiny but I know that I have faith in the One that does. The kind of faith that moves mountains!

Drum Beats

We all have our own beats that only we can hear
It is also what people feel when they come near
Our beats are what defines us, what makes us who we are
It's when we try and change them at the request of others
That we feel the same pain as being hit by a car
Those that all march to the same beat
All stumble and fall when one single person trips over their own feet
It sometimes troubles us because no one else hears it
We ask is it us or is it them when we try to understand why
Because it is important for us to fit in so we can all laugh and cry
I have learned that the beat that I hear is my very own and am now
happy that no one else hears it
So I when I hear it I know that I am home
What I can do is combine my beats with the others that I hear
To create a brand new sound together that we all can enjoy and listen
to all as one WITHOUT FEAR

Drum Beats (MP – 2012)

Business Coach | Professional Speaker | Radio Host | Author
Website: www.capbuildernetwork.com www.marceparham.com |
Email: marcp@capbuildernetwork.com

CAP BUILDER NETWORK

Marc Parham
"I Can Hear the Rhythm of the Drum"

THE DRUM I HEAR

Throughout my entire life I have always heard a different rhythm. Not only did I hear my own, I could also hear the rhythms of others. This has enabled me to easily join in their rhythm and become a part of their song.

I have been blessed with the desire and ability to help others. I received the blessing and was taught how to use faith from my family. I watched my parents make it their mission to provide assistance and change the lives of many that were directed to them.

MY CURRENT RHYTHM

I have been a consultant for over 20 years helping people all over the world start and run their own businesses. I have helped people start successful for-profit and non-profit businesses. I decided to start working on a book after listening to the questions that people ask me the most about starting a business. What I came to realize is that many people started working on their business plans and/or taking training with little progress forward and became frustrated with the whole process. What I came to realize were two important points,

One:

A great number of people lacked the confidence to get things started. They had the knowledge and experience to start a business. Only Problem?

They Don't Know They Can

Two:

Most people jumped right into starting their business without taking the time to work on developing their business ideas. Most did not do the research and development to see if their ideas would work before investing money in training and setting up the business.

As I was developing my faith mission, I realized that my entrepreneurial training came from decades of people in my own family running their own successful businesses. We sometimes forget things that we learned as a child that are still with us today. I remember at age 10 my father taking me to find my first job. Then it was a series of paper routes, door to door sales, cutting grass and many other ways that I came up with to make my own money. My brother even recalls working for me, although I think I paid him with ice cream versus real money.

My "purposed" life is to show people that they can achieve their "purposed" life by being dedicated to listening to their own beats and making sure that they use their rhythms to be in concert with others. A concert of faith.

It is also important to work with those that are willing to…

Pass The Mustard Seed!

"My mission in life is not merely to survive, but to thrive; and to do so with some passion, some compassion, some humor, and some style."

Maya Angelou

Health & Fitness Consultant | Author | Blogger
Website: www.ButterflyNotes2014.com | Email: loribmonroe@gmail.com |
Facebook: GodsGirlLove | Twitter: @LoriChiTown | Instagram: LoriChiTown

BUTTERFLY NOTES

Lori Monroe
"Know Your Seasons"

As my story goes my name is Lori but my entire family on my mom and dad side calls me Lynn, which is my middle name. They have always called me Lynn, even my childhood teachers until I got to college where my instructors started to call me Lori. That's when my first name became more active in my life. Especially as I met my husband of 27 years to date. As I've grown older, I now go by my first and middle name as an up and coming writer, mission leader and as I have developed a force of faith through my story and so Lori Lynn, it is. Thank you Lord for every one of us who are truly helping to be Jesus' hands and feet sharing His love by feeding the hungry, and spreading the gospel according to His will, plan and purpose for our lives.

I start each morning with prayer and meditation. Sometimes a short conversation with God and sometimes a long conversation with God. I give Him thanks and surrender all first thing. Truth is even after that quiet time in the morning I talk to God throughout the day finding myself talking out loud sometimes. It's real when we know that we can't do it by ourselves. Life that is. No, we cannot do it by ourselves and because God values us. I've come to know myself even more as an adult but more so when my life took a turn into a heartbreaking situation which was a setup for a comeback to Jesus circumstance. My story is in development as was my redemption. The bridge has already been built, I'm almost on the other side of it. My identity is no doubt being refreshed, renewed and refocused by the limitless power of God. I won't complain because if I looked at my roadblocks, I would never have been able to see the road...that God had already predestined for me. I've written in my journal for many, many years and Lord knows I've poured out my mind, body, soul, heart, and spirit to Him in prayer and in writing and He has poured back into me beauty for my ashes. Yes, I'm grateful.

I'm so honored to have an opportunity to work and lead a mission group with my church. Humbly and gracefully I appreciate the opportunity to minister (mission) to women in need. Shelters, Senior

Homes, Homeless people under bridges, and places that I couldn't even imagine calling it home or even laying their heads down for any period of time. My passion to feed the homeless is also a string as is my rally for breakthroughs in homelessness, domestic violence, wrongful imprisonment, rehabilitation, single parents in need, breast cancer awareness, heart disease, and that's just to name a few. I don't look for fame   or   fortune   in   any   of   it.

I walk each day as a Believer grateful that God chose me for such a task as this. Not an easy task, but He is making my mess, my message. The test, my testimony as He has chosen to use me. Everywhere I go I ask God to help me to help others, just know that it's my calling to go wherever I'm needed. I listen to God's small whispers. His small still voice. His nudges and fresh winds. I love it when I seek Him deeply no matter what kind of day I'm having. Good, bad, or indifferent kind of days. I know that they're all part of my journey. Seasons are God's plans implemented to grow us not to destroy us. KNOW YOUR SEASONS.

We must know and understand that our lessons are valuable lessons that we would never learn any other way if we didn't go through them or go through any storm or test. I read in one of my Pastor's Dr. Charles Stanley's Daily Devotional that ***"God can open windows of time, stretch our paycheck,"*** and give us victories in ways we couldn't imagine in our human thinking." Yes, I believe it. I'm a witness. God is TOTALLY   SOVEREIGN.

I also love fashion, not necessarily the trendy stuff though. Clothes are a part of who we are, how we project ourselves to the world, and make a statement about how we feel. My journey continues. I know who I am, but most importantly, I know WHO'S I am and God has built a life that is full and vibrant that others can see Him in me. Know God's purpose, plan, and will for your life. If you don't know it ask Him pray over it. God is all knowing. My greatest learning experience is along my journeys   way,   is   to   never   COUNT   ANYONE   OUT!

I'm grateful for my family, friends, and along the way some strangers who truly support me. They are all a blessed amount of my continued success. Nothing is illogical with God.

GOD'S LOVE TRUMPS ANY AND ALL LOVE.

NOTE TO SELF: Broken crayons still color. Catch the vision!

"For I know the thoughts that I think toward you, says the Lord, thoughts of peace and not of evil, to give you a future and a hope."

Jeremiah 29:11

Faith is the substance of things hoped for,
The evidence of things not seen.

Hebrews 11:1 (KJV)

High School Graduate | Founder of If You Knew Me Foundation |
Community Youth Activist |
Email: if.you.knew.me1@gmail.com | Facebook: ifyouknewme |
Instagram: ifyouknewme

IF YOU KNEW ME FOUNDATION

Kristian Munroe
"The Will to Carry On"

Faith. What is faith? The Biblical Definition of Faith is the substance of things hoped for, the evidence of things not seen (Hebrews 11:1, KJV).

I often wonder how much faith I really have because I put so much of my faith in the wrong people. To say I just "believe" is scary to me. As a teenager it's hard to believe in something that you can't physically touch or speak to. I know I may get some backlash for saying this but I feel people, especially teens are afraid to say how they really feel when it comes to faith and GOD. However, I would not have gotten this far in life without him.

My mother lives by faith. She had faith that everything would be ok when my father decided not to be in my life. My grandmother told her she would not be the first and she won't be the last and with that and her faith I am here today. When my mother drove over 800 miles to buy our first home not having a dime in her pocket, but her faith and her even surviving cancer. Faith has brought me such a long way, so why do I question it?

Growing up I didn't have much self-esteem. When they say kids can be cruel; they weren't joking. I always felt that I wasn't the prettiest, my eyebrows connected, my lips were a little bit fuller than the rest of the girls and I had thick curly hair. All of the things that made me stand out from the rest of the kids in my classes. I would try my hardest to be friendly (which meant hiding how I really felt) and that was one of the reasons why they didn't like me. When they would make fun of me I would go home and tell my mom and she would ask if I told the teacher but I wouldn't because I didn't want to come off as a tattle tale. So when my mom would come to the school and talk for me this was a way that would make it seem like it was her complaining, and then I can be like "I don't know why this lady was up here". For a long time that worked and everything was going well. The teachers and students in my class even gave me the nickname "busy", because I knew everyone's business. And, believe it or not the kids that were bullying me started to speak to me. But soon my insecurities would have a light shined on them again.

At the end of my 8th grade year I made the high school band dance line, and soon I would start my freshman year in the lime-light. They never took freshman and they chose me and another girl out of 100 girls. However, I didn't realize that I wasn't quite ready for the attention that was soon to come. I started to get the attention of a guy that almost every girl wanted and now he wanted to date me! All this time I was able to mask my feelings about my insecurities but now they were being pointed out by every girl that hated on me for being with him. And to make matters even worse, I secretly dated him behind my mother's back. I never really realized that I started to go down the wrong path; all I noticed was that my grades started to slip and the self-esteem that I was trying so hard to build started collapsing around me. My friends didn't like the way that I was acting. They said that my attitude started to change and that I was starting to be less and less happy and on top of that I was disrespecting my mother. I disrespected her so bad; I wasn't even allowed to dance at my first field performance. She then took me to the game to sit in the stands and watch my team perform on the field as a way to show me how my attitude was preventing me from being on the team that I worked so hard to be on. I was hurt, but it only seemed to hurt me for the moment. All I cared about was my man and dancing in the next performance. And in a blink of an eye that all changed. The guy I was catching hell for at home was talking about me to my face and behind my back and was now trying to talk to my close friend. The people I called "friends" soon fed into the drama and whispers. Then the year after that I was no longer on the dance line. I was devastated...maybe that was GODS way of telling me to slow down but I didn't listen.

Summertime finally came, and it was a chance for me to get away from my horrible school and social life. My mom had me volunteer at church camp and I took some classes to make up for the horrible freshmen year I had. Summer gave me just what I needed… a new start but school was around the corner and I had to get my priorities straight especially if I planned on graduating. I buckled down on my school work and tried to keep my circle small. It's strange how people can make fun of you because you want to do better for yourself. People would say I thought that I was better or smarter because I was moving ahead in my classes. So, once again I started to accommodate how other people felt, and started to hide my own feelings. I felt like I was damned if I do and damned if I don't! I started to hate school and what made it worse did I tell you my mom became the dean for my band! Thinking this would bring us closer; my mom thought that it would be a great way to get to know my friends and the people that I attempted to hang out with. Now everyone (teachers, administration, and custodians) knew who I was because my mom was here and my friends loved her being there, but I didn't.

Being the dean for the band, my mom would bring speakers to the school to talk to us about life and life choices (especially once we left high school). Even with these positive people coming to the school talking to me and my friends, even with all the teen support groups my mom put me in, it was like it wasn't hitting home for me. I felt lost. From the time I was born my mom put together "My Village". This is a group of people that have known me since birth while others came along the way to be my support team and still I had no clue. One of my problems was that I was ashamed that I was still a virgin and I planned to be one until I was married (and I still am). My peers made fun of me wanting to hold on to my virginity but that was something I was not willing to give up even if it meant not being in the crowd I was seeking. I started to lie, be manipulative, and hang with the wrong people at school. I was continuing to pick the wrong guys to like and my attitude got worse. My mom, again, got more involved and started to invite my friends to the house so she can get to know them and their thoughts outside of school.

I couldn't wait for spring break, but instead of relaxing and just hanging around the house like the rest of my friends my mom decided she was going to send me off with the church for spring break. Oh my goodness can I get a break! Even though they were going to Laguna Beach in Florida none of my friends were going! Although I thought this was going to be a preachy trip, it ended up being the best trip ever! This trip really opened my eyes and brought me closer to GOD. The GOD that I thought for years didn't know who I was; was there all along I just wasn't listening. During the trip some of the teens decided they want to take this time and get baptized. I wanted to as well, but decided to wait till I got home so I can share the moment with my mother. So at the age of 14 I decided to give myself to GOD. Here I was giving myself to GOD and thinking that my life, moving forward was going to be so much easier but instead it got harder! What everyone failed to tell me was once I gave myself to GOD the devil was going to work harder to get me back!

Home life seemed to get harder. School seemed to get harder. Friends seemed to get harder and the guys in my school were messing with my head times 10! I remembered one day going to the neighbor's house to just talk because they would always invite me to church with them and talk to me about the bible without intimidation. I was confused and I didn't understand where I was going wrong.

Senior year was pretty good. I started to get more involved in school and my schedule was lighter. I was still in the band but my mom decided not to be the "Dean" anymore as a way of giving me space but still supporting me from the sideline. My birthday was around the corner and I was turning 16! Between my mom and my uncle I had the best 2 weekend birthday celebrations ever! Shortly after that there was prom and then graduation! And after spending 3 life learning years in high-school, I graduated at the age of 16 and at 16 I am currently in my first year of college.

#IfYouKnewMe started from my own insecurities of feeling if people knew me they would know the person I really am and not the person I pretended to be to fit in. I tried to start this while I was in high school because there were people like me feeling the way I was feeling but it never got the support needed to get it off the ground. Once I graduated I started to give #IfYouKnewMe the attention needed because I still saw the need even for myself and bullying still didn't seem like it was going anywhere. It seems like when you're good people feel you don't need the attention, praise or support to continue to stay on track which does not make sense to me because in this day and age it is so much easier to stray left. But when you're doing wrong you get all the attention because everybody wants to fix you. I'm not saying that this is wrong but because we are good doesn't mean we have to be ignored!

I am here to tell you faith is hard when you're a teen and its ok if you're feeling confused about your faith. It can be overwhelming to say "I believe" but not really know what you believe in or why? I'm not perfect. I still struggle with it but I surround myself with positive people that remind me of what a loving GOD I have. With all of that said, mistakes I have made and continue to make, GOD is still with me. He made my mother never give up on me when she could have easily given up. I want to thank Ms. Lee for coming into my life and giving me so much support. I truly feel GOD brought her to me for a reason and we were meant to meet on the day we met because I almost didn't attend the Judge Penny Brown Reynolds Sister Talk Conference. I want to thank my uncle Jerome for his continuing faith in me and always telling me I can pursue anything that I put my mind too. Petrice and Marcia gave me faith to be myself and to love myself. Wendell being a single father gave me faith to believe there are good guys out there and always protected me as if I was his daughter. Sharon has 4 boys so I was the daughter she never had and could dress up. She always told me I was special and continues to be a supportive person in my life. My mom (Michelle) gave me faith because she is still here! She will always say she is not my friend but my mother and that we are married till death do us part and I will always love her for being in my corner. And last but certainly not least, God gave me the faith to carry on.

"The biggest opportunity in life is waking up!"

Yahkeem Noxx

"Trust in the Lord almighty with all your heart and lean not on your own understanding. In all your ways acknowledge him and He will create a clear and straight path"

Proverbs 3:5-6 (KJV)

Hip hop artist | Motivational Speaker | Actor | Activist
Website: www.GotNoxx.com | Facebook: GotNoxx | Twitter: @GotNoxx |
Instagram: GotNoxx

GOT NOXX

Yahkeem Noxx
"Wake Up!"

I've had to face many challenges in life, from being picked on as a kid because of my payless shoes, growing up in a fatherless home, and being recruited by neighborhood gangs. It wasn't until I was recovering in a hospital bed, fresh out of emergency surgery that I realized that the most important factor in life is having the opportunity to wake up.

While I was laying in the hospital bed, staring at the ceiling, and listening to the beeps of the heart monitor I was deep in thought thinking about all of the things I've been through in my lifetime. The ups the downs, the stupid decisions, the many times I was too close to gun fire, my most recent ex-girlfriend, my friends in jail, my friends who had died just a collage of different impactful moments from the good to the bad. I was 23 years old and most of my life I entertained the idea of becoming a professional basketball player as my ticket out of the hood. Basketball took me out of my poverty stricken neighborhood and sent me to college to experience a whole new life. I was only about 45 days away from my first European basketball camp and if selected I would go overseas and live my dream as a professional basketball player. However, God had a different plan for me. I was rushed to the hospital because I was undercut in a basketball game and suffered a shattered wrist and dislocated elbow. Lying in bed anticipating that the doctor was going to tell me I probably wouldn't be able to play basketball anymore, I was grateful that I even got to play in the first place. Plus, I knew regardless of what the doctor said I was going to be playing again. I also thought about all the people who had disabilities and never got to do half of the things I've done in life. As I lay in this hospital bed faced with a career ending injury of something I worked so hard for, for so many years I found peace because I realized I was blessed just to be alive and everything else was simply just a bonus.

Life's ups and downs often come unexpectedly, and the downs usually almost always seem to come at the worst times. We all face different challenges, endure through our own individual struggles, and battles in life; however until our final heartbeat there is one constant, that every person's pain, struggles, and challenges have in common – The blessing of waking up.

I realized that every waking moment in my life is led by choice and attitude. Every second I'm calculating decisions about something, and my attitude is the driving force that influences my decisions. The day I realized the power of perception, my life changed forever.

Many times in life we tend to let what already has happened get the best us. The longer we hold on to the inconvenience of a situation that brings us stress, the longer it takes to get back to all of the beautiful things life has to offer. I've made the choice that no matter what life throws at me, I promise to catch it with a smile on my face. The quicker I let go of the pain, stress, and frustration of the hardships of my life, I realize the quicker I could get to a solution which leads to internal peace. Now I operate with a solution based mindset, and regardless of what comes my way, I immediately seek out the solution or what can be done depending on the situation. When something bad happens in life stop replaying the situation over and over in your head, stop thinking about it don't even talk about it! All that does is allow the mental pain to dig even deeper into the ridges of your attitude and perception. Immediately start thinking and talking about what you can do about it, how you can fix it, how you can do it differently next time etc. So many people choose to hold on to the stress and pain from a situation in life for days, weeks, months and sometimes even years. Being upset and holding on to things like anger, envy, and frustration almost always fuels a bad attitude, and a bad attitude leads to bad decisions, and bad decisions lead to bad outcomes. Bad outcomes are essentially inherited by perception in life.

What you see is what you get. The power of perception can work for you, or against you. It's a choice that is primarily up to you. When you wake up in the morning choose to be happy, choose to smile regardless of what happened yesterday. Yesterday is gone, it's not coming back and there is nothing you can do to change it. Today, you can embrace the outcome of unlimited possibilities, but if you're stuck on yesterday's struggles how can you experience and enjoy today's victories? You can't, and more importantly if you start you day upset or stressed about yesterday's challenges it's a good chance you're overlooking and taking for granted the most important factor, which is the blessing of life itself. Learn to be passionate about life, and you will unlock the door to opportunity.

By becoming passionate about life, and living with a solution based mind set I have been able to overcome many obstacles that have tried to divert my path to my destiny. Finding peace in the midst of one the most challenging moments in my life helped me find the path to my purpose in life. I am now an internationally known hip hop artist, motivational speaker, actor and stewardess of life. God has a plan for each and every one of us, don't delay the route to finding your purpose by holding on to the uncontrollable events that transpire in your life. Learn to let go, and trust that God doesn't make mistakes.

"Feed your faith and your doubts will starve to death."

Unknown

Educator | Motivational Speaker | Founder of Socially Suite Consulting Agency
Website: http://www.IamAshley.co | Email: joinashleywilbur@gmail.com |
Twitter: @iamashley1218 | Instagram: @iamashley1218

SOCIALLY SUITE CONSULTING

Ashley Wilbur
"The Pressing Experience"

It had been three weeks since I had given my life to Christ. Reading my Bible and praying had become a habit, and my fascination with the mysteriousness of who God was had grown. I thought I was exempt from having problems or rough times, but I was mistaken. I was 15, mourning the death of my mother, who'd died in a car wreck three blocks down from where we lived.

She and I argued earlier that day because she wouldn't buy me the CD I wanted. I knew she was going out that night, and I wanted her to know I was sorry for arguing with her over something so stupid. The last words she said to me were, "I love you too, and I'll be back."

That night, I answered the phone to hear that she had been hurt.

"Where's my mama", I repeatedly asked the person on the phone.

My question went unanswered. I woke my aunt and grandmother to let them know what happened and did the only thing I knew to do. With my eyes tightly closed and head bowed, the words "Jesus, let my mama be all right" came from my mouth. In church, I learned that God answers prayers. He didn't that night. She was gone, and I was convinced God didn't love me.

At her funeral I didn't cry. To me, crying meant that I was weak, and I had to be strong for my younger brother and sister. On the inside, it felt like someone had ripped my heart out and stomped it a million times. She was gone, and the idea of committing suicide seemed so much easier than living the pressures of life without my mother.

Weeks after the funeral, I was preparing to cut my wrist in the bathroom and end it all. As I hung my head out the window, I noticed the flying birds. They seemed so free from everything, and that's the way I wanted to be – free.

My phone rang, and it was my spiritual mother on the other end.

"What are you doing? You were heavily on my mind, so I decided to call", she said.

Reluctantly, I told her what I was getting ready to do.

"There's a greater purpose for your life. If you keep living, God will reveal why you were created. This pressure you're feeling isn't because God doesn't love you. It's because He's preparing you for greatness", she replied. I believed her, so I put down the razor, took a deep breath and embraced the pressure.

It's been 13 years since my mom's passing, and I've learned to trust God and His process no matter how intense life gets. Although I haven't fully come into my greatness, I see myself becoming a better me. I'm still in the race. My goal every day is to show up and keep moving with the end in mind. Life isn't complicated. In fact, it's quite simple.

Making the decision to change how we perceive our circumstances determines if we win. Life is a strategic teacher. It seeks to mold us into our best selves through a multitude of changes, a series of tests and a calculated balance of highs and lows. With no preparation at all, we are given situations that introduce us to our strengths.

I named these circumstances the *"Pressing Experience"*.

A vital lesson can be learned from something as simple as the diamond and the olive. Under extreme pressure and heat, a chunk of coal transforms into a diamond. As for the olive, it is valued for the precious oil it expels under intense stress.

When you find yourself going through the *"Pressing Experience"*, keep in mind these seven vital tips:

1. Choose to endure.
2. Don't throw in the towel.
3. See the beauty of your situation.
4. Have patience with yourself and with God.
5. Appreciate the journey and the transformation of your true self.
6. Find the lessons in your circumstances.
7. Be willing to share your story. It may save someone's life.

Above all else, keep the faith when everything around you is in complete chaos.

"Feed your faith and your doubts will starve to death." – *Unknown.*

"When your heart is right with God and your desire is to please God. God is obligated to bring you into the company of the people that you need to know, the knowledge of the things that you need to know, that is critical to your success and destiny in life."

Robert King

Public Speaker, Business Growth Strategist, Radio Personality
Website: www.robertking.info | Email: robert.king9044@sbcglobal.net |
Facebook: Overcoming Broken Trust

SBC GLOBAL

Robert King
"Overcoming Broken Trust"

TRAIL
"Of my Life"

Overcoming trust can be the most rewarding feeling after you have allowed forgiveness to replace bitterness, anger, confusion, frustrations, un-forgiveness, and other emotions that attempt to consume you. Allowing God to heal you from the inside out takes time in order for you to effectively help others overcome broken trusts. For me, it all began May 15, 2013 after returning home from a 30 day trip to Indiana to take care of my ailing mother. I discovered my wife of eight years had been having an affair and had actually brought her lover into our home and marital bed.

Confusion gripped me because we were pastors of one of the fastest growing churches in the Southwest Florida area which was founded February 2008 and had experienced great blessings from the Lord only to later be shut down within 90 days. Divorce had been mentioned; however, I never saw myself disconnecting from my wife whom I truly loved. I don't want you to think everything was her fault; therefore, let me assure you that I wasn't perfect as a husband or pastor; however, I was faithful. It felt as though a domino effect had taken place in my life because many had walked away during the biggest storm in my entire life. In all of this, I wondered, where was the love of Christ?

Prior to this I had considered myself a faith giant. Everything I had accomplished had come from my ability to target my faith and belief. Now even my faith had been shaken. I felt that God had abandoned me. I felt like He had completely went silent on me during this enormous trial. But it now reminds me of the saying that, "Teachers are normally quiet during the test." I questioned God as to why He didn't protect me from this excruciating pain, embarrassment, criticism, and persecution? But I now realize that I had to go through it to come out of it.

TURMOIL "Fight for my life"

Discovering broken trust, can at times send you on an emotional roller coaster. You may experience the highs, lows, dips, twists, loops and the worst feeling is not knowing when it will stop. During this ride you will cry, laugh, scream, yell, and yes maybe vomit. The question is, do you stay there or fight for your life, your joy, and you inner peace? There are many stages to this process; therefore, please allow me to explain these four stages to you:

HURT:

The very moment you discover the broken trust you will feel the emotions that come from being hurt. This phase of the process has to be dealt with seriously because many people are hurt because everything they believed in the areas of love, commitment, loyalty, faithfulness have been shattered. If this stage is not dealt with swiftly it can be followed by depression, suicidal thoughts, or actual suicide, promiscuity, guilt, shame and embarrassment. In my personal experience and years of counseling as a pastor people who are hurt and betrayed by close love ones often want to lash out and hurt those who have caused them pain. This is surely NOT the answer.

HATE:

This stage of the emotional roller coaster can be extremely dangerous due to hate towards their unfaithful partner. Many are not thinking suicide, but homicide. I don't say this lightly or in a joking matter because many have inflicted bodily harm on themselves and others due to unfaithfulness. It's an emotion that can creep up on you when you least expect it regardless of your spiritual, emotional, or educational strengths. As much as you can't fathom you hating the person you once loved, when hurt and betrayal from that person are combined, hate attempts to creep in; however, you don't have to allow it. During this stage not only did I begin to hate my unfaithful partner, but I also didn't want to hear from God. Although the Scripture says: he will never leave you nor forsake you, but I felt God had left me alone. You may find yourself looking for confirmation, more proof, and an apology. Looking for the why they cheated. But it's not worth it; therefore utilize that time and energy on healing and seeking God.

HEALING:

It's Ok to not be Ok. In other words don't beat yourself up if you haven't gotten there yet. Better to arrive when you're supposed to and receive true healing then rush it and not truly be healed. Move on cautiously and carefully praying for guidance because you can and will love again. After interviewing with surviving Overcomers it is said that the residue of discovering broken trust is always present and can be triggered at any moment if you allow it to do so. Remember, you are aiming for true peace in your heart and mind, not revenge. The good news is you can be happy, emotionally healthy, and that to me is healing. *Rose Kennedy quotes: "It has been said, 'time heals all wounds.' I do not agree. The wounds remain. In time, the mind, protecting its sanity, covers them with scar tissue and the pain lessens. But it is never gone."* When it comes to healing it is my experience that time is simply designed for this purpose.

TIME: To Improve My Emotions

Over a period of time, and that time will vary from person-to-person, you will gain more control over your emotions as it relates to broken trusts, remember it's a process. Some days are better than others as you regain control of your emotions. Overcoming broken trusts also requires recognizing "Trigger Points".

TRIGGER POINTS:

You know, seeing your unfaithful partner, dropping off the kids, running across an old picture whatever it may be. Brace yourself and say, let's go. Whatever you do don't beat yourself up for still having those emotions during these "Trigger Points". Remember it's a process and eventually one day even those trigger points will have less of an impact on your life and that overcomer is healing in the process.

HAPPINESS:

Thank God you have made it this far to the pursuit of happiness. I believe happiness comes from your ability to allow God to heal you in order for you to one day share yourself with someone else. Happiness is attainable, after having gone through your broken trust situation, through faith. What does that mean? It was my ability to reconnect and reestablish my relationship with God during my most difficult time which reignited and replenished my faith. I write, not through teardrops but pen drops expressing to you how to be able to say:
I will love again, I will trust again, I will be loved again, I am valuable, I bring a lot to the table, and I am marvelously and wonderfully made! I am smart, I am beautiful, I am deserving of the best, and I am faithful.
I'm very happy and the thing that gives me so much joy, is the ability to *Pass The Mustard* Seed on to you and once you have made it through your experience, I encourage you to *Pass The Mustard Seed* as well.

TRIUMP "Passion of my life"

It is vitally important that once you have completed the overcoming broken trusts process that you ask God to give you what I call the 3P's. What Positive, Purpose can come from this Pain? The positive, purpose from my pain was what ultimately birthed the Harmony Holmes and Adult Family Care Home. Not only is the Florida home being transformed into a place for seniors to live out the rest of their lives with dignity and class, but it is an entire training system. When your heart is right with God and your desire is to please God; He will open doors that no man can close and He will heal your heart in ways that no one can. Birth positive purpose out of your pain, then you will have gained a lifetime of wisdom for you to pass on the mustard seed of faith for healing to someone who is overcoming broken trust.

"And YHWH said, Behold I have given you every herb bearing seed, which is upon the face of all the earth, and every tree, in which is the fruit of a tree yielding seed; to you it should be for food."

Genesis 1:29 (KJV)

Certified Holistic Nutritionist | Vegan Chef | Health Consultant | Hip-Hop/Spoken Word Artist | Actor | Director | Fashion Designer | Photographer | Teacher
Website: www.NEHZAHR.com | Facebook: Nehzahr | Instagram: Nehzahr

NEHZAHR

"Healing & Enhancing"

Flashback. 2002. My father, Ricky Lovely, drove himself to a St. Louis Hospital after getting off from work. He says he wasn't feeling good, but this particular pain was something he'd never felt before. His body shut down and he was barely able to walk. After being checked, it was determined and prescribed that my father had Kidney Disease and was on the verge of death. This day would change our lives forever.

For the upcoming New Year some friends and I decided to eliminate pork and beef from our diets. At that time, we were researching and studying a lot of cultural and intellectual based books seeking to find a better over standing on who we were as a people, and what we are supposed to be doing in life. We felt we had to stop eating pork and at least beef to get to a higher consciousness. Both of my parents were from the south, so I had eaten everything from raccoon, to duck, chitterlings, frog legs, pig snoots, pork skins, liver, chicken gizzards, hog head cheese, and even sea roaches{shrimp}.Taking these things away from everything else that I ate would be a challenge, but I was definitely up for it. Although years later through extensive research, I learned that chicken and fish was basically the same thing as pork and beef. Meat is meat. After 2 ½ weeks, I instantly dropped close to 10 pounds, and I wasn't even working out in those days. Maybe this new diet was working, or maybe by eliminating pork and beef, I also was losing unwanted fat! The more I became health conscious, the more my father became sick. He was losing weight and his energy levels were decreasing daily. By this time, he was going to dialysis 3 times a week, and it was taking a toll on him.

I was still eating chicken, fish, and turkey 2 years after cutting out the pork and beef. I felt like I was healthy and planned on continuing through life eating "white meat". Dialysis was beginning to consume my father and this man who I held so high, who did karate, ballet, enlisted and did 2 separate terms in the military, boxed, played basketball, lifted weights, and ran was breaking down right in front of my eyes. There are hundreds of diseases and cancers that stem from animal based diets and

Kidney Disease is one of them. The dialysis procedure goes as such: your body is hooked up to a machine through an open wound somewhere on your body{ on his arm}, then all the blood from your body goes into the machine, "filtered", and then put back into your body. Totally unnatural.

Yes my father was in great shape, but he wasn't making the right food choices. So it was only natural that, what he was eating, our family was eating as well. There would be times when he would come home from dialysis, and then 10 minutes later, completely black out and collapse. Whether having a conversation, sitting at the kitchen table, or even walking up the stairs to get to the front door, he would just black out. Enough was enough! This would be a key moment in my life that would change history forever. I told myself that I was going to break the cycle that was set before me. I'm no longer going to eat what generations of people before me were eating. If, and when I have children, I didn't want them to see me go through what I saw him go through. You have to be spiritually and mentally strong at a young age. Everybody can't handle that pressure. I was unsure if he was going to wake up after he blacked out. So in the summer of 2005, I promised and vowed never to eat or drink animal products again.

Fall 2006. Moving to Atlanta was one of the best decisions I could've made in life. My brother and I moved away from East St. Louis to get way from all the madness and malice that was infecting that area. There was plenty of opportunity to make money, and get some sort of notoriety with our music, and Atlanta was also a place where there was plenty room for growth. However, after a month, the $1000 we had was virtually gone due to eating every day, transportation, and extended stay hotels. Not to mention, the fall season was comfortably sitting at cold every day. We spent our last few dollars on a hotel room on Memorial Drive in Decatur. We stayed there a few days praying that we would get a call from one of the many job applications we filled out. But no one ever called. It was freezing and pouring down raining the night we had to be out of the hotel room. I knew the clerk at the desk and he let us stay a few hours past check out time without jeopardizing his job. My brother was ready to go back home. There was someone on his phone willing to buy us 2 bus tickets home. The only thought in my mind was, "Look, I've come too far just to go back to a place where death is on every corner." The St. Louis area was only profitable for a certain "class of people" and I wasn't making any money or could get a job. "You can go back, I'm not going, I'll sleep on the streets", is what I told my brother. A certain look of surprise had overcome him. He knew I was serious. He knew he would have to stay too. He knew he couldn't leave.

Sleeping on the streets was like nothing I could've imagined. Atlanta was approaching its coldest days and the only warmth we got was from riding the Marta train all day. We could've gotten robbed at any moment. We could've gotten arrested at any moment. Being a Vegan was the last thing on my mind. By this time, I'd eaten Little Debbie Snack Cakes, hamburgers, beef stew, Churches Chicken, and even Thanksgiving Dinner from the Hosea Williams Feed the Hungry. It was survival of the fittest and I wasn't too arrogant to eat meat. I had to do what I had to do. For 2 ½ months, we slept in parking garages, playgrounds, tar fields, U-Haul Driveways, and the woods behind someone's house. Taking a bath/shower wasn't even an option. But we stayed strong and steadfast in our prayers, knowing that better days had to be coming. Eventually we both got jobs. He at Arby's and me at Checkers. Working at Checkers gave me easier access to food and I knew it would only be a matter of time before we saved up enough checks to get our own place, which we did. My Creator provided, and I was open to receive the blessing. I wasn't ashamed of eating meat based on the reality we were facing. Now, I can get back on my feet.

8 Years Later. I'm still standing strong today. I live a totally Holistic Lifestyle. I've been a complete Vegan since living on the streets, I exercise daily, and I have a Holistic Nutritionist Certification.

I'm a Vegan Chef, Health Consultant, and have dedicated countless years of research and studying, always seeking new and innovative ways to live longer, and younger through a Holistic and anti-death lifestyle. I went from eating every kind of meat you can name, to every kind of fruit and vegetable you can name. After years of consuming garbage, and with the torcher done to my body, I was able to heal myself through diet/nutrition, now focusing on the enhancement of all the vital vitamins and minerals that I'm taking in daily. It took years to get here. But it was all baby steps. I embraced the challenges. I didn't give up. I planned, I pursued. I started a new generation of Vegans. I'm healing people. I'm enhancing the earth. By the way, my father, he's still living today and just turned 60. The life expectancy for a dialysis patient is 7 years, and he's been on it 12 years.

After years of listening to the doctors telling him he needed meat, he's subscribing to a healthier lifestyle and getting stronger by the day. The goal is to eventually get him off of dialysis. Never give up the fight and the will to live to fully manifest and transcend to who you're originally supposed to be!

"Sometimes what makes us insecure and vulnerable becomes the fuel we need to be overachievers. The antidote for a snakebite is made from the poison, and the thing that made you go backward is the same force that will push you forward."

T.D. Jakes, *Reposition Yourself: Living Life Without Limits*

Women Ambassador | Girls Advocate | Author | Founder of Tween Star Awards
Websites: www.shekinamooreETC.com | www.tweenstylepower.com |
www.tweenstarawards.com | Email: info@tweenstylepower.com

TWEEN STYLE POWER

Shekina Moore, Ed.S.
"Owning My Voice Took Faith"

So you want to know my truth? The truth is I was in no ways the bold visionary woman I am today. For a long time I lived in a self-imposed frustrated and unfulfilled shell of a life. I used to have this nagging habit of wanting to please people and I had to have two, three, sometimes even four people to co-sign anything I did. This could be anything from what should I wear to the event or to who should I partner with on this project. Grand ideas would be birthed in me, but I was so paralyzed by the thought of failing and disappointing people that I often completed little to nothing at all.

The problem was I lacked two things—confidence and FAITH. To deal with the confidence I had to peel back some layers to see where all the self-doubting was coming from. I figured if I could face my past that I could gain control of my future.

For a long time I really did believe that being a female was holding me back. I believed that in order to lead, I needed to be packaged differently. It was a lie and it wasn't until I faced that truth and sought mentors in my life that I was released from that mindset. Once I renewed my mind, the world began to open up to me.

How can I apply faith to my daily journey? Your faith simply helps you to see beyond the difficulties placed in front of you. So what can you say to remind others to walk by faith and not by sight?

Sometimes all you know is what you see as faith is a muscle that must be employed and trained. You must guard your ear and eye gates, protecting them because environment matters! This is why our girls must be exposed to all the possibilities without limitations of gender. When glass ceilings are presented to them they have to be taught to see beyond the false presentation and into the unchartered.

EMPOWERING GIRLS COMES FROM A DEEP PLACE

In early 2013, I was inspired to start pouring into girls like never before. It was something I wanted to do where girls could bond and grow into leadership with the freedom to ask questions, speak up and shine (not things traditionally learned in school). For a long time it was something I ran from because it meant I would have to articulate what always bothered me growing up—invisible women. Looking at some of my experiences, it's no wonder I was inspired to create a platform for girls to shine; to be celebrated; to be seen; and to be valued.

Growing up, I never quite felt that I was valued because I didn't see many matriarchs esteemed or their voices heard. Being a female, it seemed was for the pits. Value seemed to always be placed on the male position. At least that's how I saw it then. As a matter of fact, when I looked at most women, they seemed to be so different from me. I couldn't relate on a deep level. I felt confused by why I wasn't domestic enough or happy serving and letting *men be men*. Back then I really didn't quite know how to articulate my frustration but today I do. I saw so much in myself but I was crushed that no one else "got it". I recall excelling in Business class and I wanted to be a business woman but in my core I didn't think I was good enough. I went to school on a Business scholarship and I still didn't think I was good enough. Wow!

Some of my fondest memories were of the Sundays when we would have these big dinners and lots of laughter. However, there was always what dishes to wash afterward seemed like a gazillion. My brother never had to help clean up. I remember thinking how unfair it was that I had to do the dishes because I was a girl. I even recall mumbling under my breath every time I had to wear a skirt to church even when I was cold. Though no one ever explicitly said you are doing these things because you are a girl, it was always implied.

Fast-forward, I was that newlywed in the kitchen rolling my eyes every time my mom would ask me if I was going to fix my husband's plate. I wanted to fix it because I wanted to, not because I was a female and that went with the territory.

Today, I know the uneasiness I felt stemmed from these narrow definitions of what it means to be a female. They made me feel second-class to men. With so much to offer beyond those definitions, it seemed I wasn't packaged right. I didn't want to offend anyone with my VOICE which left me feeling empty. I believe this empty feeling was the start to my journey to being a girl's advocate. Having to deny my voice to fit this notion of a girl's proper place eventually had to come to a head.

Interestingly, once I found my voice, I became that business woman I always wanted to be. As for my husband, turns out, he never really cared for my fixing his plate. I have a great respect for the old school where survival was the name of the game. Growth is a beautiful thing. As you grow, the picture gets clearer. I am at peace knowing that owning my voice is giving other girls permission to own their own without apology.

Owning my voice took faith; faith that everything would be alright if I bucked the status quo as so many before me did in their own way. So, there you have it. Me, authentically, female.

Shekina Moore, Ed.S. is a Girls Advocate dedicated to empowering girls with positive body image healthy esteem and leadership tools. Learn more about Shekina at www.shekinamooreETC.com.

I will remember the Lord my God, for it is He who gives me Power to get wealth so that He may establish His covenant that He swore to my forefathers.

Deuteronomy 8:18 (KJV)

Travel Consultant | Contributing Author
Website: www.townsend-enterprises.com | Email: michelle@njoytravelgroup.com |
Facebook: michelle.townsend.904

TOWNSEND ENTERPRISES

Michelle Townsend
"Opened Doors"

And so it began, July 17th 1961 I; Michelle Julia Townsend was born to Ron and Barbara Townsend in Queens, New York. Growing up in a 2 bedroom apartment in the Big Apple taught me how important it was to stay focused and never give up. My mother and father worked hard to provide for my brother and I the best way they knew how.

Life changed for me at the age of 9 years old when my parents separated. Being one of the only kids in our neighborhood that didn't have a two parent home wasn't easy. I knew that I always wanted something better out of life and wanted to do everything in my power to make it happen.

My senior year in high school I found myself facing more adversity when my science teacher told me that I should take up a trade because I wasn't college material. This was a turning point in my life and I made up in my mind that I would prove him wrong. Not only did I attend a private University, but I graduated in four years; isn't God Good!

In 1985, I moved to Atlanta for a better quality of life and to strengthen my walk with Christ. I joined Ebenezer Baptist Church the same year and this is where my faith journey began. The following year I entered into marriage and gave birth to a beautiful baby girl.

In 1991, I found myself as single parent and was determined that I wanted my daughter to have a better life than I did growing up. By the grace of God I was able to make sure that she received the best education possible.

God opened many doors for me in the corporate world along the way. September 11, 2001 changed the world; December 11, 2001 changed my life. I walked into work only to find out that my services were no longer needed. I had been laid off and found myself asking God what should I do? I was head of household, with a child in private school, and a mortgage to pay; I had no idea how I was going to survive.

After depleting my savings account and my 401K, I needed another stream of income to replenish what I had already spent.
Eight years ago a dear friend of mine Sherrie Massie presented an amazing recession proof business opportunity that just made sense.

I will remember the Lord my God, for it is He who gives me Power to get wealth so that He may establish His covenant that He swore to my forefathers **(Deuteronomy 8:18).**

Being involved in the largest industry in the world has been a blessing beyond measure. Warren Buffet stated; "If you use it and it makes sense you might as well own it," and that's exactly what I did. This business has allowed me to double my monthly income as well as show average individuals how to earn above average income.

"A Good man leaves an inheritance to his children's children. **(Proverb 13:22)**

As a business missionary, I'm on a crusade to take back the body of Christ one family at a time. It's An Amazing World and You Must See It!

"It is your faith that moves mountains, not your hands."

Author Desiree Lee

Author | International Public Speaker | Mentor | Disabilities Advocate
Website: www.IamLakisha.com | Author Email: authorlakishalouissaint@gmail.com

I AM LAKISHA LOUISSAINT

Lakisha Louissaint
"Greater Heights"

Big things happen to little people who were once considered failures. Your dream is not a competition, it is simply a destination. After dropping out of high school my senior year, I dreamed of failure, I ate failure, and I danced/waltzed with failure daily, but after being encouraged that I too could succeed, I realized that it was time to kick failure to the curb. I refused to allow shame and embarrassment to consume me and I conquered fear of failing and became a GED recipient. Later I enrolled into college facing all obstacles that were placed before me. Knowing nothing of writing papers frustrated me; however, I never knew it was the challenge that was preparing me for greater. I never enrolled into college to become successful, I only enrolled to prove a point, but even in that God knew that it was preparing me for my future. My English professor and spiritual mother encouraged me along the way. They planted seeds because they believed in me. The problem was that I had to believe in myself and I had to have faith in God.

As a senior in college with a 3.3 GPA, having to sit out of school for the purpose of advocating on behalf of my son's education, due to Autism took me back to a place of failure. My perception of life was distorted by the opinions of others and it seemed as if all hope was lost. Failure stepped in as I was dancing/waltzing with faith and reached for my hand and I began dancing with failure yet again. As faith stood by and watch me dance/waltz to a song of pity, it interceded on my behalf and reached for my hand, but this time I was determined that failure would not return because of my new ability to believe God regardless of what it looked like. God used what the world considered a statistic and deemed useless because of my faith and allowed me to succeed even though I believed I had failed. God didn't give up me and He placed others around me to push me further than I believed I would go. Statistics symbolizes you in a sling shot and every time something comes to push you back, it is God preparing you for a take-off that will lift you to heights no man can take you. Therefore, when shame and embarrassment comes; replace it with faith, when you fall; get up and don't allow dropping out of school to weigh you down. Don't allow the opinions of others who suggest that you will never be anything suffocate the life out of your dreams. Get up, hold your head high, and take a step out on faith, because faith without works is dead. The question now is, does one give up on their dreams because they never walked across that stage to earn their high school diploma or a degree? No, it simply allows God to use the simple to confound the wise. Someone once said, "You have to know that you know that when God tells you that there is greatness inside of you, that it is really there." So, will you sit and allow someone's opinion of you make your dreams lay dormant inside of you or will you have faith that God can do exceedingly and abundantly above all you can ever ask or imagine?

No one ever thought that a little girl who was repeatedly told she would never be anything would turn out to be an author, advocate, and inspirational speaker, but I did. Regardless of what anyone has spoken over your life to discredit who God says you are, you can still achieve your dreams. Be determined and understand that life is only what you make of it. You can wallow in pity or become all that God has called you to be. Remember, a double minded man is unstable in all of his ways. Big things __DO__ happen to people who were once considered failures.

When you get to that starting line don't panic, just remember, this is not a competition, it is your ability to reach your destination without fear of failure. *Ecclesiastes 9:11 gives a very true statement, "The fastest runner does not always win the race, the strongest soldier does not always win the battle, the wisest does not always have food, the smartest does not always become wealthy, and the talented does not always receive praise. Time and chance happens to everyone." (NCV)* In other words, the race is not given to the swift, but to those who will endure to the end. Being a high school dropout or one without a degree, does not disqualify you from succeeding, your inability to believe and have faith does. Your perception of yourself should be one of positive thoughts. You are not a failure you are a success. You have to perceive to believe that you can do anything because your faith lies in God, not a degree.

I am Lakisha Louissaint and I never gave up, I stood in the face of adversity, and I realized that although I didn't succeed as fast as others, God was propelling me to heights, I thought I would never reach and now

I am passing the mustard seed on to you as you seek to see your dreams come true. Remember, greater is He that is in you, than He that is in the world.

"When thou pass through the waters, I will be with thee; and through the rivers, they shall not overflow thee; when thou walk through the fire, thou shalt not be burned; neither shall the flame kindle upon thee."

Isaiah 43:2 (KJV)

Drug & Alcohol Treatment Specialist | Author | PTA Board Member | Motivational Speaker | Addiction Counselor
Email: mccauleyenterprise@gmail.com | Facebook: Anthony McCauley

MCCAULEY ENTERPRISE

Anthony McCauley
"Not My Attitude, but My Reaction"

In order for me to accomplish my dreams I had to overcome a stronghold of drug abuse and alcoholism. This writing is inspired by actual events of my life and personal struggles that had to be dealt with in order for my life to change and a developing of my soul to take place. Recalling times when I found myself in uncomfortable situations and dark places, this journey has been one of stupidity, loneliness, manipulation, accomplishments, addiction, highs and extreme lows. Finding ways to discharge discomfort while knowing I am hard wired for struggle, but also worthy of loving and belonging, thriving for a sense of realness and authentication. I found myself always tempted by the shiny apple and eating of bitter fruit, longing for a world of truth, always trying to find a way to beat the system without having any debts to pay, but I quickly found out all that you have is your soul! I had to deal with the attitudes and behaviors that kept me from moving forward and reaching my goals, figuring out what was weighing me down!

How do I breakdown these cultural norms associated with addictive behavior. Dealing with life on life's terms made me realize that family and good friends are essential. Throughout my struggles I found myself continually praying and asking God why me? Why want you help me? You said "you would never leave me nor forsake me", I am loosing respect Father, respect for myself and other people rights. The perception of myself was continually fading because of this vicious cycle of addiction. At the age of 17 I turned my life over to God and I was saved! Not knowing that this was the best move I could ever make because there was something different about me, a sense of wanting to know more about God, but I have this relationship with drinking and using drugs. My Aunt Lula B. Spencer (R.I.P) was a God fearing, Holy Ghost filled saint of God who truly lived and worshipped God in a way that you very rarely find in the body of Christ these days. I must give her accolades because not only at an early age did she pour into my life, even when I found myself in the midst of dark foolishness, she reminded me to remain faithful and look to God for strength, constantly telling me I was going to be an effective witness of the overcoming power of God and I would one day "Pass The Mustard Seed"!

I remember talking with her in small short conversations about real issues, she knew indirectly my struggles with alcohol, tending to catch me with a glass in my hand! She could look at you and you would instantly sober up! The power of God was all over her, and now I know what she meant when she said "the battle is not yours, you just need to make up your mind to serve God and when you do, and people will not understand you." I kept no secrets from her because she could get a prayer through and her comforting words always assured me this too shall pass, I always let her know I am trying to stop acting like a fool in the streets drinking and using drugs, well let me be specific cocaine.

The importance of letting you know about her is significant to who I am today. I want you to know I have been on the front line of battle in a world that leads to gutter experiences and horrible pit surroundings, don't get me wrong along the way I have achieved major accomplishments while in the midst of active addiction, there where breaks and clean times; however, once I took that first drink it was the jump off to achieve the ultimate "high" which by the way will never happen! I guarantee before you think you will get there you will experience jails, death, and institutions! I realize I was allergic to the lifestyle because I always broke out in handcuffs!

I came to find out that alcoholism and drug abuse lead to brain damage. Our bodies are designed to operate on what we have been given at birth. When you incorporate mood altering chemicals your emotional state of mind is changed and you are now experiencing a feeling of euphoria that leaves your body saying "whatever that was give me some more of that". You see, not only did cocaine overload my dopamine receptors but I grew accustomed to blowing them so far off track, that I begin to fall in the stereotypical name calling associated with my disease, like drunk, crack head! And the way I carried myself on the streets, those around me in certain places had the audacity to say "we don't consider you a crack head you just a smoker you go to work every day" WHATEVER!! I was losing my mind and barely hanging on to job opportunities that always led to termination.

I have been blessed with two beautiful daughters Tamaria and Marissa who I always had an indirect relationship with due to this disease of addiction, totally exhausted my marriage and I take full responsibility for not stepping up and being the man that I should have been to cultivate what God blessed me with. This is just an avenue to give you a piece of my story, I had faith throughout the past thirty years, but only if I could just see beyond this and have a moment of clarity I would be ok, but my faith wavered so badly off track.

I pray that you feel the overcoming power and faith I maintained to get to this point and know the only limits you have are all in your mind. It is in you to prosper and imagine your possibilities, you must have that "mirror" experience. If you can honestly love the person looking back at you, then good for you; however if you look in the mirror, you are not the fairest of them all.

Immediately rearrange and realign your life to match the life that God has in store for you. I so love looking in the mirror, because I truly love what I see! I have applied to my life the outlook of believing something good can happen. It leads me to continue in ministry, just becoming more effective by loving God and others has been the transformation that I needed to come back from a dead situation. I have not arrived and this is something that I must work for at the rest of my life! I have to attend outside support groups where I find people just like me, I have to have an awareness that at any time I can go back. The fact that I can express myself and love myself keeps me motivated to help those that have lost hope and feel all alone.

I have learned to live life without any mood altering chemicals, so if this touches only one person then my labor is not in vain, so I pass the mustard seed and in my fearless pursuits I will embrace what's next! My prayer is that this book gets to the right person and the power of God will give you the faith to have a moment of clarity to overcome and break free from the vice that is binding you. Just know I have faced some challenges that made me realize it wasn't my attitude towards addiction, it was my reaction towards it! I want to leave you with this and if you have to read it over and over you will get knowledge for your situation.

Father God, I thank you for increasing our faith. I plant this writing as a seed for those that will pursue their education on purpose. I pray that the finances will be readily available and scholarships will be awarded.
Father, I thank you that our young people will defy every odd and pursue their goals. Father I pass the mustard seed to the next generation

I thank you for the harvest!

In Jesus Name, Amen.

College Success Coach | Teen Mentor | Founder of Education on Purpose
Email: bcollegeprep@yahoo.com | Facebook: eopurpose

B COLLEGE PREP

Nichole Brown
"Education on Purpose"

As we all know, after high school comes the real world; therefore, preparing our youth is crucial. As each student propels to heights of success, it gives me great joy knowing that I played a part in planting seeds of wisdom into their lives. I remember this organization asked me to facilitate a workshop once a week for 6 weeks. I was so excited! I had been given the opportunity to work with high school seniors whom had excelled academically; therefore, I figured it would be a smooth breeze. But that fantasy quickly became a reality once I realized the students had no idea what they wanted to do after high school. Many of the students spoke of their faith and how they encouraged others, but they lacked faith in their own ability to have success.

During the workshops, we discuss the importance of financial aid, scholarships, how to get books, etc… As we all know, finances are one of the reasons why students do not graduate. Well, many students have enough faith to go to college with the minimum, but later are impacted by the lack of finances that help with the necessities needed for college. Scholarship success searches require faith. I am determined to help this next generation see that applying for scholarships is essential to college success. Normally, students look for scholarships as the last resort; however, those results can be detrimental. Many scholarships are available the junior and senior year of high school, but the student must put in the work to find those scholarships because they don't always knock the your door.

I've worked with a student who had not applied for one scholarship by January of their senior year of high school. The one day this student called and I explained to this student that some scholarships were still available and immediate action was needed. The student had to continue applying not knowing if they would be selected. All the student needed was faith and because of their faith, we devised a strategy and this student became a finalist and eventually won over 10,000.00 in scholarships!

I also remember a student who didn't have the finances needed to stay in college. They never had all the textbooks so they would borrow other students' books after hours to study. They would try to be first on the library list to check out textbooks. This student had to rely heavily on their notes from class and every word the teacher said. Imagine taking tests and barely seeing the material yet still getting passing/excelling. The student refused to give up in the face of adversity and graduated on time within four years.

One of the students from this workshop maintained a 3.75 GPA throughout high school. It was now preparation time. The student was informed and prepared to take college entrance exams and apply to colleges. The student later graduated from high school with honors worked at low paying jobs and regretted never seeing where their scholastic ability might have taken them. Many students may feel they are not college material; therefore, affecting their decisions to move forward. Regardless of the situation, it is vitally important to encourage each student to secure academic success through the power of faith in order to see their dreams become reality.

As each challenge presented itself during the workshops, my faith grew stronger. I was not willing to give up on the students or allow them to give up on themselves. Each student overcame many obstacles to attend college and earn their degrees. Enrolling into college is one thing, but encouraging them to not give up is another; therefore, I set out to encourage each student by saying, "You will finish" Regardless of the crisis that presents itself. I made myself readily and available to the students and developed strategies which in return produced college graduates. Many of the students are now living their dream life!

All each student needed was faith the size of a mustard seed to help them realize their dream. It warms my heart every time a student graduates because I know the obstacles they have had to overcome. I'm on a mission to encourage students to go to high school on purpose, pursue higher education, to become college graduates, and productive adults. My faith was increased throughout this process to keep encouraging students to add purpose to their education. Now, I pass the mustard seed on to you!

You can't save the world hanging out with people
Who live to destroy it! Reshuffle your inner circle and
Watch your potential become intentional.

Bob Mackey

Founder of M Powering Choices | Founder & Facilitator of Power of the Knot, the Power of the Purse | Motivational Speaker | Author | Youth Mentor |
Website: www.mpoweringchoices.net | Email: propersonalities@gmail.com |
Facebook: mpoweringchoices

M POWERING CHOICES

Bob Mackey
"(B.O.B) Bring Out the Best!"

Growing up I had nothing but a smile. Many times, I'd watched that dwindle away and become a constant struggle to keep it! The pipeline to positivity was on a lite bridge crossing over a group of negative family members and others who cared less about my life or my future.

I prayed daily to escape from a place of no return but for some reason, I found inadequate reasoning that was placed on a lonely freeway forbidden by a sign reading no way out. How could this happen to me? I asked! Well, living to learn was the complete opposite of learning to live. Having no active father and seeing a part time mother, I made many mistakes without adult supervision. I wasn't a bad kid, but for the most part. I was outstanding! In school I was on Honor Roll, an avid helper, and a kid that would do anything to help anyone but yet, I was labeled a problem child because I was young, black, and gifted! Something that many schools had little to no experience working with; that is young males who fell in this category. It was difficult to attend school daily afraid of being misunderstood. I was far from dumb but didn't take kind to people who tried to belittle my ambitions just because of my last name, MACKEY.

Eventually, I quit school but never quit learning and was forced to slang dust not really, but I thought it was a way to an understanding since many of the fella's I rolled with made a way. Then it hit me......I recalled something that a gentlemen told me, He said" You can either be outstanding or out there standing." For once in my life I realized that I was out there standing and it was not where I was supposed to be or where I wanted to stand. As the rapper Jeezy said, "I remember nights that I couldn't remember nights saying to myself I had to get it right." I was so disappointed in myself. I could only think about the people that I would prove right. So much potential but nothing was intentional. As time moved on I had to consider my options but I had none.

Despite my odds, I remained optimistic and found a construction job! I kept clinging on to the little faith that I did have. So close to the bottom but not far from the top is how I would describe my life at the time. I knew that I was supposed to be someone. I knew I had purpose & passion! But, it seemed as if faith was the only thing that I could walk around with and it was not ashamed of me. And with that faith, I noticed how kids would always flock to me! I could be one out of one thousand and somehow all of the kids would be in my corner, seeking my attention of playful soul.

As much as I ran from it, it eventually found me. Finally it happened, I decided to answer a call that I had been sending to my voicemail for the longest. My faith had lead me to answer a call that would change me and my life forever. After no consideration…I begin working with youth! And, some forty-thousand youth later…I've been able to believe, achieve, and inspire a new beginning. Faith moved those mountains and left enough hope on the table to start over without regrets. Doors began to open and I had a chance to close a few shut.

How did I do it?

Faith and Aspirations! Believing and knowing that what was in store for me could not be taken by those who did not give to me. I positioned myself to reconstruct my life and completely changed my mindset. I learned to B.O.B (Bring Out The Best) my head to a different beat. From my hair, to my shoes, I had become a new person! I was someone that many feared I would find but I started to see more people who loved me than those that hated me!

You're going to have people who will not believe in you, belittle you, and chastise you! But, you must not stop because your dreams are much larger than those people. No kidding, my biggest critics were my relatives yours may be as well. Whoever it is, it is not your struggle to own! You were made out of greatness so greatness you shall become!

How could this be?

"Edward Everett Hale stated that "I am only one, but I am one. I cannot do everything, but I can do something. And I will not let what I cannot do interfere with what I can do." Our society continues to make it seem that everything is okay! However, this past decade, we've experienced extraordinary growth and changes in our society in regards to the development of our youth. Within the past years, juvenile delinquency has seen an increase from youth between the ages of 7-16. The Justice System is no longer seen as a rehabilitation center for young people but as a reformatory that entitles behaviors that are unacceptable in society. Action is needed! Now is the time to ignite life-changing programs that will bring about change to our youth around the world. Which led me to discover my gifts of impacting our youth's lives through educational development.

My organization is called, M-Powering Choices. M-Powering Choices, Inc. is a non-profit organization created to design and present programs to young men and women that will empower them to make responsible choices in their lives. M-Powering Choices targets all young men and women, with a special emphasis on "at-risk" individuals, from the third through twelfth grade. The programs emphasize making responsible choices, such as dressing responsibly, which in turn leads to positive performance in the classroom and ultimately a successful life. These programs impact the participants in their everyday lives and build character, self-confidence, self-discipline and self-respect.

Our vision is to build character through education and appearance. **We're also here t**o increase young people's awareness on the importance of character, appearance, and education that assures success while developing the "IQ, I Can, & the I Will" and demonstrating good values which promote students making healthy decisions as a part of their lifestyles.

We've sparked a movement and we're ambitious with a purpose. Living off of faith and driving with passion is how we roll, but we also know that we can't do this alone. We're here to share a community vision that will enable action steps to achieve success and change lives as we move forward with partnering efforts. We have essential knowledge, experience, and expertise in working with youth; especially at-risk youth who are long overdue for an opportunity to consider change. The connection between effort and extraordinary is the dedication that great folks like you and all who give daily.

We must build up our youth to reach for the impossible… even in turbulent times. I was lost without a plan. But, someone took the time and effort to ensure that my potential would be more than potential. There's so much to be done! We help youth understand that "The Way They're Dressed Determines How They're Addressed." And, it's not where you start but how you finish the race that matters the most. We hope that your will, will make a way! The Power is Within You! Every Source Is Not A Resource!

*"Thoughts become things. If you can see it in your mind,
You can hold it in your hand."*

Bob Proctor

Founder of My Wall of Dreams | Online Marketing Consultant | Contributing Author
Website: www.mywallofdreams.com | Email: crystal.scretching@gmail.com |
Facebook: MyWallofDreams | Twitter: CScretch | Instagram: CrystalScretching |
YouTube: MyWallofDreams | Google+: +CrystalScretching

MY WALL OF DREAMS

Crystal Scretching
"Thoughts, Feelings, Actions"

Thoughts become feelings | Feelings become actions | Actions become results.

Have you ever done something you were not proud of? I remember around 9 years old being invited to one of my friend's birthday parties. For obvious reasons, I had no money so my mom had to buy, and in turn, pick out the birthday present. I hated this! I wanted to gift my friend something from me that was special. I kept thinking about this and wondering how I could get something for my friend with no money. The day of the party, we went into a store to pick up a card to go with the gift we bought. My mom also decided to browse a bit since we had time.

I walked around the store eying all kinds of things that could have been better presents than what we had gotten. Then, I spotted a flower that was so pretty and my friend's favorite color. As we walked around the store, I kept looking at it, wondering if I should ask my mom to get it. I knew she wouldn't though. We already had something for the party. When we were checking out I felt myself slowing slipping closer to the flower. Before I knew it I had swiped the flower and walked out the door with my mom.

I couldn't believe what I had just done! I have never stolen anything before and knew much better, that this was wrong to do. Being young, I thought this was just me being impulsive and out of character for good reasons. Long story short, I didn't get over my mom with the story of "I just found it!" and had to take it back.

But looking back on this now, I realize that this act was not impulsive because I had pondered over the thought in my mind for a prolonged period of time before even going into the store.

This is how we are in many areas of our lives. We get results we are not pleased with and never realize the foundation of what got us there in the first place. This story is lighthearted just to make a point, but there are far worse and detrimental situations we end up in, only to realize how deep it is when it's already too late.

Thoughts lead to feelings. Feelings lead to actions. And actions lead to our results. Thoughts shape our world. This is why it says in Romans 12:2, "...be ye transformed by the RENEWING of your mind..."

This is the reason we often fail when trying to make a change in our lives. You see, we must first win the battle in our minds before we can even begin to see actions. Taking on change without first getting your thoughts in line is like running out on the battlefield with sword and armor without taking the training classes on martial arts and proper equipment use. The odds are against you.

And this is not a lesson of just choosing between wrong and right. This applies to everything in life. If there is a job you are wanting, don't defeat yourself in the mind before you even get an interview. Those negative **thoughts** will turn into strong **feelings** of self-doubt and discouragement. And you still may get the interview, but then your **actions** during it may show your doubt and lack of confidence. **Resulting** in the employer losing confidence in you and passing you up to go to another candidate.

This is why we must be mindful of our thoughts, because whatever your mind has been conditioned to believe about you and your blueprint towards life is what has been shaping your world thus far. So *affirm* your world. Talk to yourself! David had to encourage himself and I now understand this more than ever because no one can do it for you. Outside of praise, encouragement and accolades will only get you so far and last so long. You have to be self-accepting. When everyone is gone at the end of the day, you have to live with yourself and your choices.

I encourage you this entire week to filter your thoughts with the visions of whom you see yourself as and how you see your life, even if you aren't in those positions currently. Then reject worrisome thoughts and anything negative that tries to break this thought pattern. Watch how much your world changes around you.

I speak on this not as a concept, but from personal experience. The moment that I became aware of my thoughts; was the moment I began to take charge of my life. I switched from being a bystander of what was happening in my life to creating a life filled with purpose and passion. I turned off the negative noise that would tell me "You're not good enough" and embraced the power placed inside of me by God. I know in my heart that all things are possible, but it first begins in the mind.

CLOSING REMARKS

"From Desiree Lee"

Now that you know have realized that you are not alone while walking through your journey. Know that you have the power to create your own wealth, the power to use the tools given to go beyond life's most difficult barriers, and the will to not give up in well doing.

While you are going through, take this time during your dark place to prepare for the opportunities that await you. You wouldn't want to be caught standing face to face with what you've have been longing for all of this time and haven't taken the necessary steps to embrace it, once it has been offered to you.

Do the best you can with what you have until you can do better. The best feeling in the world, is when you are presented an opportunity and you are prepared. No longer look at your glass as half empty, instead look at your glass as it is half full. Look at your dark place as your season of preparation, and every season has a harvest. If you will make a conscious decision, just as the contributing authors did during their darkest hour, to work a little bit at a time towards your dream, towards your goals, towards your vision. Eventually, you will reach greater heights. Remember this, it's not your environment that dictates your success, it's your mind.

IF YOU DON'T LIKE YOUR HARVEST CHANGE YOUR SEED.

ABOUT THE AUTHOR

DESIREE LEE

Best Selling Author Desiree Lee is a California native, a living example of overcoming personal experiences with a criminal background, low self-esteem and defeat. Ms. Lee also reveals in her first book *INMATE 1142980: "The Desiree Lee Story"* about a lady with the mustard seed which changed her life. This experience has inspired her to write and publish *Pass the Mustard Seed*. A renowned keynote speaker, author, and philanthropist, Ms. Lee shares her story to audiences across the country. She has shared the stage with Judge Greg Mathis at Praying for Our Children Winter Gala, in Orlando, FL; National Coalition of 100 Black Women in Chattanooga, TN; Judge Penny's Sister Talk Conference in Atlanta, GA.

She has also used her radio and television interviews to introduce a youth and parent mediation service that helps parents and their children better communicate. Parents have applauded this because for many it has opened lines of communications that had been virtually shut down. Her public speaking engagements have been well received and in a short period of time she has become a well sought after motivational and inspirational public figure. Many organizations working with young people are excited about Author Desiree Lee. They seek opportunities to introduce their audiences to someone with a real story, about a real experience that has made a real change and is impacting communities nationwide.

Founder & Creator of 10 City Prison Prevention Tour | Best Selling Author | Inspirational Speaker | Philanthropist | Author Workshop Facilitator
Website: www.DLeeInspires.com | Email: d.lee7211@gmail.com |
Facebook: dleeinspires | Twitter: dleeinspires | Instagram: dleeinspires

MEET OUR CONTRIBUTORS

OUTBANDING JEWELRY

Outbanding Jewelry, brings Taliyah & Brianna's creativity to life and to you! Two young entrepreneurs found out that they didn't have to wait to begin living their dreams. Sisters Taliyah & Brianna, create bracelets, charms, necklaces, and rings with rubber bands. These young girls took what they loved doing and cultivated that into a business in a matter of weeks. The Atlanta community saw what they were doing and wanted to support them. Before they could even make it to local events they were already bringing in a profit. Their parents Roderic and Naomi supports their vision with marketing, branding, and daily operations. Taliyah and Brianna both want to see Outbanding Jewelry reach its full potential into something that can expand beyond retail and transfer into other fields such as motivational speaking and entertainment.

Founders of Outbanding Jewelry | Young Entrepreneurs
Website: www.outbandingjewelry.com | Email: outbanding@gmail.com | Facebook: Outbanding Jewelry | Instagram: Outbanding Jewelry

CHRISTA WILLIAMS

Christa "K" Joy Williams is a native of the Augusta, Georgia area and has lived there since 1982. She attended and graduated from South Carolina State University with a bachelor's degree in Family & Consumer Sciences/Business in 2007. Since 2010, Christa has been in the beauty industry as a Beauty Care Specialist with a multibillion dollar company that has been growing strong since 1963. Her passion for motivating and inspiring people in her community to become extraordinary and healthier individuals led to her current career in radio broadcasting.

Christa is currently the Director of Administrative & Support Services at WNRR Gospel 1380 AM located in North Augusta, SC. She is also the Executive Producer and Host of her weekend radio broadcast "The Beauty Essentials Show". This radio ministry discusses topics such as: fashion, health, beauty tips, relationships and spiritual growth. Christa "K Joy" has had the distinct honor and pleasure to meet and interview celebrity entertainers, music artists and public figures such as: Real Housewife of Beverly Hills Kyle Richards, Taffi Dollar, Wife of Creflo Dollar, Celebrity Makeup Artist and Beauty Expert to A-List celebrities and major beauty corporations, Julianne Kaye and much more.

Christa's background and focus on community collaboration has led her to a number of volunteer opportunities, community leadership roles and partnerships. Christa will also receive her Graduate Degree in Human Services Counseling: Life Coaching from Liberty University located in Lynchburg, Virginia and her Professional Certification in Fashion Styling and Master Makeup Artistry from QC Makeup Academy. Her favorite quote is: "Be the change you want to see."

Radio Executive Producer & Host | Beauty Care Specialist | Public Figure
Website: www.thebeautyessentialsshow.com |
Email: Email:beautyessentialsbraodcast@gmail.com |
Facebook: The Beauty Essentials Show | Twitter: @b_essentials4u |
Instagram: thebeautyessentials | YouTube: Christa Williams Beauty Essentials

Nedra Buckmire is a multi-gifted speaker, workshop facilitator, co-pastor, mentor and certified professional life coach. She is a native of Brooklyn, New York but currently resides in Georgia. She is employed as an Executive Administrative Assistant to the Chief Human Resources Officer for a large multi-media entertainment organization headquartered in Atlanta, Georgia. In addition to functioning in the area of administration, she also assists her husband of 24 years, Curt Buckmire, in ministry as co-Pastor of Spirit and Truth Worship Center located in Loganville, Georgia. She received her Bachelor of Arts Degree in Leadership and Administration from Beulah Heights University and is a certified professional life coach with Dream Releaser Coaching (DRC). With a passion to empower others and a special heart towards women, she has founded Extraordinary Women Ministry which is called to empower, equip and encourage teens, young adults and women to walk in their God-ordained purpose. This ministry exists to inspire hope, ignite passions and rewrite futures.

Co-Pastor | Mentor | Certified Professional Life Coach | Workshop Facilitator
Email: nbuck390@gmail.com | Facebook: Nedra Buckmire | Twitter: @nbuck390

DAN MOORE, SR.

Dan Moore, Sr. is a Philadelphia native and accomplished filmmaker. He served as an Executive Producer for WXIA-TV, an ABC affiliate in Philadelphia. He has established several successful film companies and produced films in West Africa, one of which was on Liberia's President, William Tolbert.

His film credits include writer, producer, director, cinematographer and editor. He has filmed a short documentary for Bill Cosby and produced films on the legendary football great, Gayle Sayers and Tony Award winner, Melba Moore. Moore has worked with Cicely Tyson and Ossie Davis as narrators in his projects.

He has authored more than 10 books and is the founder of the APEX (African American Panoramic Experience), Atlanta's Black History museum, and several other nonprofit organizations.

Dan Moore, Sr. Founder/President APEX
African American Panoramic Experience Museum
135 Auburn Ave, Atlanta, GA 30303
Website: www.apexmuseum.org | Email: apexmuseum@aol.com |
Facebook: Apex Museum

TWIN OF A KIND FOUNDATION

Twin of a Kind is an organization based on building self-esteem and creating positive self-awareness by motivating and encouraging youth/young adults to see their potential. A hallmark of TOAK is gaining self-acceptance and the understanding that everyone is different in their own way. Twin of a Kind provides interactive workshops called "Unlock and Unleash Your Star Potential" designed to help individuals get to know themselves, love themselves, and be true to themselves.

Twin of a Kind takes you as you are; caters to both male and female, ages ranging from 12-24. The dynamic, twin duo utilizes their professional work experience in mental health, modeling, and real-life lessons to engage participant interest. Twin of a Kind is well-positioned to provide services to the following:

- Faith based Organizations
- Non-Profit Organizations
- School Districts
- Conferences & Expos
- Youth Based Organizations
- Mental Health Agencies
- Park and Recreation Department

Twin of a Kind is preparing to officially launch in early 2015 a spectacular community event that caters to youth and creating a platform for individuals to unleash their star potential.

Celebrity Models | Public Figures | Twin of a Kind Foundation |
Workshop Facilitators | Motivational Speakers
Website: www.twinofakind.org | Facebook: Twinofakind | Twitter: @twinofakind |
Instagram: @twinof_a_kind | YouTube: Twinofakind1

LAWRENCE "POP" RUTHERFORD

POP | POET OF PEACE, born Lawrence Charles Rutherford II, hails from Atlanta, GA by way of Anchorage, Alaska. Growing up POP won hearts and entertained family with his "old man" personality and style so much that he was nicknamed "Pop." Little did he know his nickname would soon reveal his purpose as the evangelistic poet, POP | POET OF PEACE. After answering God's call in 1999, POP has gone on to write numerous poems that have blessed countless hearts and led to many lives being saved. POP frequently ministers through music, poetry, and the arts at jails, nursing homes, and youth detention centers in an effort to win souls for Christ and uplift those too often marginalized.

A true renaissance man, POP is also an established author, music producer, song writer, and composer. His book, Planting Seeds for the Lost & Found, is a masterpiece frequently hailed as a "Poet's Bible." The work simply but masterfully marries poetry with vivid artwork, Scripture, and profound wisdom to bless Christians, non-believers, and poetry admirers alike. POP is currently promoting his upcoming CD, Lyrical Witness, which is set for release fall 2014.

Author | Poet | Music Producer | Song Writer | Composer
Website: www.poetofpeace.com | Email: pop@poetofpeace.com |
Facebook: Poet of Peace | Twitter: poetofpeace | Instagram: poetofpeace | YouTube: Poet of Peace

Everyone has a unique life story to share – but at one time, Javona Smith's life was filled with hardships and challenges. Javona survived violently abusive relationships and drug-infested neighborhoods. She was emotionally, physically, verbally and sexually abused over the years. The personal trauma, inappropriate exposures, and poverty-stricken conditions that Javona identified as a normal were all she knew. Consequently, she was pregnant at 15 and homeless at 19. Instead of accepting the life it seemed was dealt to her, eventually Javona rewrote the pages of her own life. Now she has overcome all of the obstacles that at one time held her back and is helping other women heal from their past. Javona Smith is the founder of a PR & Publishing company that will help play a huge role in helping other ordinary women share their extraordinary stories.

Women's Mentor | Author | Motivational Speaker | PR & Publishing Owner
Website: www.JavonaSmith.com | Email: admin@javonasmith.com |
Facebook: JavonaS

NICK BARTLEY, M.ED.

Nicholas "Nick" Bartley, M.Ed. is a serial entrepreneur with 15+ years of "qualified" experience in meeting/event planning, graphic design, brand management, and business development consultation. He is a native of Savannah, GA and a product of the Chatham County Public School System completing the Business, Legal, Financial Magnet Program at the Savannah High School and pursued a B.S. degree in Mathematics from Morehouse College, an M.Ed. degree in Educational Leadership and a Certificate of Hospitality Administration in Trade Show and Event Planning, both at Georgia State University. He served in professional capacities as Budget Assistant, Budget Analyst and Director of On-Campus Recruitment & Special Events all at Morehouse College prior to venturing into the entrepreneurial journey and is now Founder/CEO of The V2L Corporation and Executive Director for Program Administration for Alliance of Dreams, Inc. Currently, he resides in Atlanta, GA and is a proud member of Kappa Alpha Psi Fraternity, Inc. and a devoted member at New Faith Mission Ministry (Griffin, GA) where he serves on the Finance Team and is Director of Media & Marketing.

Founder & CEO of The V2L Corporation |
Executive Program Director of Alliance of Dreams, Inc. |
Brand Management | Business Development Consultant
Website: www.NickBartleypresents.com | Email: nick@V2Lcorporation.com |
LinkedIn: www.linkedin.com/in/nbartley | Facebook: V2Lceo | Twitter: V2Lceo

DEMARLO WEST

Makeup Scientist was born and raised in Milledgeville, Georgia. Academically, he received his B.A. in Sociology/Criminology from Paine College in Augusta, Georgia. After graduating from Paine, DeMarlo attended Troy State University in Troy, Alabama and received his Master's degree in Education with a concentration in Counseling/Psychology. DeMarlo began his journey of enhancing natural beauty in 2006. His motivation and mission was to ensure that clients not only look beautiful, but also feel and understand the essence of beauty captured within them. He is well known for conducting "Tour of Tutorials" throughout the USA and abroad. His tutorials have equipped clients with the skill set to execute soft editorial looks, to evening glam. DeMarlo has five (5) apprentices under his tutelage, coaching and inspiring makeup artists to achieve their maximum potential. DeMarlo has worked with celebrity clients such as Donald Lawrence & Company, Jonathan Nelson, Blanche McAllister Dykes, VaShawn Mitchell, Pastor Paula White, LaShun Pace, The Anointed Pace Sisters, LaTrice Pace, Monica Lisa Stevenson, Lacretia Campbell, and many others.

Visual Beauty is the simple most important element in the Law of Attraction. So when clients are looking to be enhanced, exaggerated, and modified, they look to DeMarlo West. The Makeup Scientist is detailed with an eye of perfection. He has strategically found a way to not only enhance natural beauty but also create illusions in experimentations. A Scientific Genius that's creatively brilliant.

Shadow Designs LLC is a freelance makeup company that provides cosmetic services to both genders and all cultures. We are committed to enhancing natural beauty with a simple, clean, and classy approach. From your initial point of interest, to the conclusion of rendered services, it is imperative that your experience with us is exceptionally professional and beautifully unique.

Founder & Owner of Shadow Designs LLC | Celebrity Make Up Artist | Make Up Scientist Workshop Facilitator
Website: www.demarlowest.com | Email: info@shadowdesigns.org |
Facebook: DeMarlo West | Twitter: makeupscientist | Instagram: makeupscientist

TEKA DOWNER

After experiencing the darkest chapter of her life, Teka Downer emerged motivated, inspired and "reinvented." She never imagined such pain would give birth to a revelatory movement and encouragement to the masses. A movement she calls Re-Me which is short for Reinvent Me. She gathered every drop of that inspiration and poured it into Re-Me, the book. A 15-day devotional to spark your journey to a better, brighter you! Teka has over 10 years of training and facilitation experience which she has allowed to become her platform for motivational speaking. She is known across the state of Georgia for her high energy and out of the box approach to engage, educate, and empower individuals through whatever training she conducts.

Teka brings a sense of fun and purpose to her work with youth and adults alike, using result-based facilitation that encourages organizations to achieve at their highest levels. As a Consultant, she strengthens the bonds of relationships in the workplace and often encourages staff to identify and appreciate their differences that stronger workplace relationships might be formed. She is a graduate of Georgia Regents University and past Assistant Director for Columbia County Community Connections; a state-wide collaborative for the state of Ga. Teka is now a consultant and specializes in Leadership Training, Program Development, and Results Based Facilitation. As a contracted consultant, she has trained for The Department of Education for the state of Georgia, The Governor's Office of Children and Families, and The Georgia Bankers Association. It is her desire to motivate and inspire all.

Author | Leadership Consultant | Workshop Trainer | Public Speaker
Website: www.remeteka.com | Email: ReMeTeka@gmail.com |
Facebook: TekaDowner | Twitter: ReMeTeka

DENISE BRASWELL

Denise Braswell, has spent the last 25 years as a wife, a mother and business owner which hails from Freeport Long Island. She with her husband Pastor Mark they have two children, Amber and Ryan. Denise and Mark met in undergrad where they both attended Virginia Union University. After getting married the two moved their young family to the metro Atlanta area where Mark Pastors a local Ministry.

Denise currently owns and operates The Haven Learning Center. The Haven is an academic support service program which provides, private school education, tutoring, before and after school services and an academic summer camp. The Haven Learning center also conducts ACT/SAT Prep courses. The Haven has been a thriving entity for the past eleven years.

Denise believes that perseverance is the key of her on-going growth and development. It has allowed her to become better at what she is called to do.

Owner & Director of The Haven Learning Center | Education Coach|
Website: www.thehavenlearningcenter.org | Email: thehavenlearningcenter2821@yahoo.com |
Facebook: TheHavenLearningCenter

ALTWAUN NELSON

Altuawn Nelson is an independent film writer, director, and producer. He specializes in offering solutions to some of the issues that urban youth are faced with: drugs, guns, gangs, bullying, peer pressure, parenting, conforming to a criminal lifestyle, and sexuality. Being raised in a lower socio-economic community in Southwest Atlanta, he's able to relate with many of the plights that drive inner city youth to commit crimes.

He founded "From Nothing to Something Productions" in 2012 to release youth oriented films. "The Alto Adjustment Documentary" was their first film, which is based on the life of Dainhen Butler who is a reformed felon. Altuawn is also the host of "The From Nothing to Something Show" and part owner of E3TV, which streams on Roku and Google TV.

Co-Owner of E3TV | Independent Film Writer | Director | Producer
Website: www.fn2sproductions.com | Email: fntwos@gmail.com |
Facebook: Altuawn Nelson | Twitter: @altuawn1 | Instagram: altuawn_nelson

As one of the nation's up and coming thought leaders, Life Strategist, Entrepreneur and Author, Jessica Anderson is changing the lives of youth and young adults attempting to go against the grain in today's society of unhealthy relationships, low self-esteem/ low confidence, learning to follow their dreams and walking in purpose. She is the author of a soon to be released book titled *Shades of Me*, which gives you an in depth and transparent look at her life and the decisions she made as a teenager that forever changed the course of her life.

Atlanta, GA native, Jessica attended Fort Valley State University. She completed her undergraduate degree prior to moving to San Antonio, TX. While in Texas, Jessica took a large leap of faith and followed her dreams of becoming an entrepreneur and founded Glamorous Events, LLC, a full service, boutique event planning & consulting firm.

Knowing that she was called to do more and serve in a larger capacity, Jessica began to serve in various arenas that she felt led. It wasn't until she shared part of her personal story with a group of people that she realized her life journey was meant to be shared with the masses. Driven by faith and dedication to service, Jessica serves on numerous boards including the **National Black MBA Association (San Antonio Chapter)** and as a Texas Fellow for the **League of Young Voters Fund**. She has worked with various organizations including the **NBA** and **NFL**. Jessica believes in strengthening the esteem of young ladies while uplifting and educating them to be the best person they can be for themselves, and has committed the use of her voice and life experiences to make it happen.

Glamorous Events, LLC Founder | Author | Event Planning & Consulting Firm Website: www.theglamqueen.com | Facebook: theglamconsultants | Twitter: @glameventsceo | Instagram: jess_speaks_life

DOROTHY "PENNY" JONES

Dorothy Jones, born in Chicago, Illinois is the owner of 'Be Whole...Mind, Body and Soul, LLC'. Personal trainer by day, she is an advocate of healthy living, and encourages everyone to take care of their bodies through physical training and daily exercises.

For the last 8 years she has served as the Minister of Dance at Prevailing Love, located in Stone Mountain, GA, where she birthed *Ambassadors of Christ* from very humble beginnings to a powerful group of young women who understand the power of the ministry of dance.

She vehemently believes in the power of the word of God, and relies upon it heavily for strength and encouragement. Her favorite scripture is Proverbs 18:16, "*A man's gift maketh room for him, and bringeth him before great men.*" She is a living testimony of God's gift making room for her.

Minister of Dance | Personal Trainer | Healthy Living Advocate
Website: www.djones.weareboss.biz | Email: Djones@weareboss.biz

Marc E. Parham is a business coach, professional speaker, radio host and author of the book "Yes I Can – Develop My Idea and Start My Own Business". He has been working for over 20 years to help people start and grow businesses. His mission is simple, to educate and coach people to start taking more control of their lives by learning how to start their own small business.

Marc is a Managing Partner at the CAPBuilder Network Group; (www.capbuildernetwork.com) a consulting company whose focus is helping people start and grow their own businesses. He is also the creator the successful business information site called The CAPBuilder Network (www.capbuildernetwork.com) and radio show CAPBuilder Talk (www.capbuildertalk.com) that provides articles, information and resources to help start and grow small businesses. On October 11, 2013 Marc was invited and attended a meeting with President Obama to discuss how the shut down and debt ceiling issues were affecting small business. The meeting was held at the White House and it was co-sponsored by Business Forward. Marc, a member of the Business Forward Local Leadership Council was one of a select group of nine individuals invited to attend the meeting.

Business Coach | Professional Speaker | Radio Host | Author
Website: www.capbuildernetwork.com www.marceparham.com |
Email: marcp@capbuildernetwork.com

LORI MONROE

A Chicago native and now a resident of Atlanta, Georgia; Lori Lynn Monroe is an author, wife, mother, compassionate mission team leader, health, and fitness consultant. Mrs. Monroe met her husband during college in 1985, which their union has grown gracefully throughout the years. With their two children Jeraad and Tayler Jade Monroe.

Lori has found that the lessons during her seasons has led her to the passion for helping others. She strongly believes that it's all about the journey, God's will, plan and purpose for her life. With her faith, she is committed to help others to enjoy their journey while accomplishing their goals.

Health & Fitness Consultant | Author | Blogger
Website: www.ButterflyNotes2014.com | Email: loribmonroe@gmail.com |
Facebook: GodsGirlLove | Twitter: @LoriChiTown | Instagram: LoriChiTown

Kristian Munroe is originally from Brooklyn, New York but moved to Georgia when she was about 10 years old. She graduated from South Gwinnett High-School at the age of 16, and is currently in her first semester of college. Often bullied about her physical appearance, Kristian from young wanted to understand why. So, instead of talking with her fists, she spoke with her mouth, using this as a better way to handle confrontation. In doing this she realized that the people bullying her were either going through something or was ashamed of their own imperfections and feared people bullying them. Oddly enough, a lot of Kristian's bullies became people that she could talk to, continuing on to present. Making Kristian hope that if you open the lines of communication people will realize that we're not that different from each other.

With that being said, Kristian started **#ifyouknewme** amongst her friends and family, to help make a difference in her community and in our teens, because she personally knows how it feels when someone makes you feel unworthy. Her goal is to keep the conversation going, because bullying is not going to stop because she says so, or because October is anti-bullying month. We need to let people know if you're going to continue to keep bullying us as a community and a generation will keep talking.

High School Graduate | Founder of If You Knew Me Foundation | Community Youth Activist |
Email: if.you.knew.me1@gmail.com | Facebook: ifyouknewme |
Instagram: ifyouknewme

YAHKEEM NOXX

Christopher D'Angelo Williams better known as "Yahkeem Noxx" realized his true calling in life, to motivate and inspire the world as a motivational speaker, actor, hip hop artist and activist. He also works behind the scenes as a photographer, videographer, and film editor.

With relentless drive and ambition, Noxx had found major success after several years of commitment. He currently serves as the Production Manager on the award winning stage production, Rimshot Urban Musical, the Creative Director on the critically acclaimed stage production "The 11th Hour", and managing partner for The Positive Arts Movement. Noxx is not only known as a game-changing hip-hop artist and actor, but he has become an inspirational motivational speaker and activist. His unique approach and delivery captivates both youth and adults with messages that always hit home and inspire.

Hip hop artist, Motivational Speaker, Actor, Activist
Website: www.GotNoxx.com | Facebook: GotNoxx | Twitter: @GotNoxx | Instagram: GotNoxx

ASHLEY WILBUR

Ashley Wilbur is an educator, a motivational speaker and the founder of Socially Suite, a Social Media consulting agency. A native of Chattanooga, Tennessee, Ashley graduated from Howard High School.

With hard work and dedication, she paid her way through college and graduated from Fisk University with a Bachelor of Arts in English. At the age of 22, Ashley kept her promise and returned to her alma mater, Howard High School, to become an English teacher and athletic coach. After 6 years of dedication, she took a position at Tyner Middle Academy in Chattanooga, where she currently serves as the Reading Specialist. Ashley's teaching style is relevant to today's youth. She can be characterized as a stand-up comedian crossed with Oprah Winfrey. Her style of teaching challenges young people to become long life learners while on the pursuit of discovering their own identity and purpose. Ms. Wilbur believes that teaching what you love and sharing what you know opens the gateway to unexplored worlds.

Educator, Motivational Speaker, Founder of Socially Suite Consulting Agency
Website: http://www.IamAshley.co | Email: joinashleywilbur@gmail.com |
Twitter: @iamashley1218 | Instagram: @iamashley1218

ROBERT KING

Robert is a highly sought after Speaker, Business Growth Strategist and Radio Personality. He has been successful in prospecting, starting and growing businesses for over 30 years. Over these years, he was pivotal in the success of varies businesses including real estate, network marketing, financial services, salon ownership and church planting.

In an effort to assist business owners in starting, staying and succeeding in ANY type of business, Robert King, Master Prospector, conducts workshops to provide strategies on immediate revenue growth. His workshops will provide basic fundamentals often overlooked but needed to get the exposure every business needs to help propel their business' growth.

As an experienced master prospecting coach and trainer, he conducts workshops on various topics including: How to Prospect to grow your business, Church Growth Strategies, The Lost Art of Face to Face Prospecting and Small Business Growth Strategies.

Birthed from a personal experience Robert is the creator of the movement Overcoming Broken Trust "It's a Process". He ministers to broken people all around the world who are dealing with overcoming someone breaking their trust through infidelity. His Facebook private group Overcoming Broken Trust is rapidly growing and impacting lives daily. As a former founding Pastor his ability to relate with hurting people and redirect their faith has become an incredible healing combination. As a man of Faith Robert believes *Everyday above Ground Is a Good Day* and there is nothing you can't do if you put your mind to it and apply corresponding action.

Public Speaker, Business Growth Strategist, Radio Personality
Website: www.robertking.info | Email: robert.king9044@sbcglobal.net

NEHZAHR is a married father of 2 beautiful boys, Yakir-age 2, and Ahkiyah-age 6 months. He is a Certified Holistic Nutritionist, Vegan Chef, Health Consultant, Hip-Hop/Spoken Word Artist, Actor, Director, Fashion Designer, Photographer, and Teacher. His 1st Album, "Hakatsah" is out right now and has received critical acclaim from all ages and nationalities of people. He is also currently starring in 2 theatrical productions," Rimshot the Urban Musical" {voted Atlanta's Hottest Stage Play} and The 11th Hour. His company, Healing and Enhancing, focuses on diet, nutrition, exercise, meal plans, catering, and a host of many more things to save your life. NEHZAHR'S family is entirely Vegan, and he definitely plans on having more children so that they may go forth and sow sacred seeds for generations to come.

Certified Holistic Nutritionist | Vegan Chef | Health Consultant | Hip-Hop/Spoken Word Artist | Actor | Director | Fashion Designer | Photographer | Teacher
Website: www.NEHZAHR.com | Facebook: Nehzahr | Instagram: Nehzahr

SHEKINA MOORE, ED.S.

Pegged a Women Ambassador and Girls Advocate, Shekina Moore has dedicated her life to their empowerment. Shekina believes helping to develop healthy esteem and positive body image in girls is the key to tapping into their leadership capacity. She holds three degrees and has worked extensively in the school systems of North Carolina. For a long time Shekina did not have a voice. All the years working with youth, Shekina began to notice that girls really did not have a voice. Too often, we fail to recognize girls for their invaluable contributions, placing too much emphasis on their physicality. One day Shekina watched a documentary on girls that sparked something in her. Where are the voices? Who is standing up for our girls?

Shekina is the visionary behind the Tween Star Awards™ that is showcasing and celebrating tween and teen girls who are shining in their communities, making valuable contributions. A six-time personal development Author, Shekina was named one of 52 Empowering Women Who Empower Girls along with The One World Doll Project's Stacey McBride-Irby, HGTV Property Virgin's Egypt Sherrod and WNBA President Laurel Richie. Featured in a host of publications, radio and TV shows, Shekina was also selected as a national semi-finalist for Proctor & Gamble's My Black Is Beautiful Ambassador Search (2014) and named Who's Who in Black Atlanta (2014).

Women Ambassador | Girls Advocate | Author | Founder of Tween Star Awards
Websites: www.shekinamooreETC.com | www.tweenstylepower.com |
www.tweenstarawards.com | Email: info@tweenstylepower.com

Eight years ago a dear friend of mine Sherrie Massie presented an amazing recession proof business opportunity that just made sense. Being involved in the largest industry in the world has been a blessing beyond measure. Warren Buffet stated; "If you use it and it makes sense you might as well own it," and that's exactly what I did. This business has allowed me to double my monthly income as well as show average individuals how to earn above average income. As a business missionary, I'm on a crusade to take back the body of Christ one family at a time. It's An Amazing World and You Must See It!

Travel Consultant | Contributing Author
Website: www.townsend-enterprises.com | Email: michelle@njoytravelgroup.com |
Facebook: michelle.townsend.904

LAKISHA LOUISSAINT

Lakisha Louissaint is a native of Troy, Alabama. She learned early, that in life we all go through difficult challenges, but Lakisha Louissaint found strength in God through it all. She was no longer bullied by her tears and became the author of *Tears of Silence* which tells the story of her life. She boldly takes a stand against molestation, high school dropout rates, promiscuity, and the misconceptions of pregnancy and disabilities. Encouraging our youth to no longer be paralyzed by fear and have the courage to conquer their past, present, and soar like eagles into their future. Lakisha is an author, international speaker, mentor, wife and the mother of two teenage boys, one in which is diagnosed with Autism. Providing the essential tools needed, Lakisha is an advocate for those living with different abilities ensuring that they receive the Free Appropriate Education designed just for them. Lakisha is on a personal mission to help others triumph over the tears that are drowning them. Ms. Louissaint has no intention to stop, until she has reached every individual young and old that is patiently waiting for her mustard seed.

Author | International Public Speaker | Mentor | Disabilities Advocate
Website: www.IamLakisha.com | Author Email: authorlakishalouissaint@gmail.com

Anthony B. McCauley is a native of Thomasville, NC. He is the eldest son of Bernard and Mary McCauley, and also a graduate of Thomasville High School where he excelled in academics as well as athletics in three varsity sports. After overcoming his own personal bout with addiction, Anthony has completed vocational training as a Drug and Alcohol Treatment Specialist and continues to work towards educating those who still suffer with the disease of addiction. He is involved as an active member of the Thomasville High School PTA board. Anthony is currently pursuing educational goals at Southern New Hampshire University in Manchester, NH completing requirements in the field of Psychology concentrating in addiction counseling. Anthony also has goals of going national with a message of experience, strength, and hope. By serving as a member of Toastmasters International he has been given the opportunity to enhance his public and motivational speaking skills by completing different levels of speaking competency with the organization. He is also involved in the outreach ministry at Connections Church of Thomasville with future sights set of ministering to others.

Drug & Alcohol Treatment Specialist | Author | PTA Board Member |
Motivational Speaker | Addiction Counselor
Email: mccauleyenterprise@gmail.com | Facebook: Anthony McCauley

NICHOLE BROWN

Nichole Brown is a college and career coach who has helped numerous students pursue their college and career goals. Her motto is that every student obtains the ability to walk in purpose. She accepts the challenge to work with every student. Ms. Brown is determined to influence the next generation to strive for success. She believes, if college is your choice then why not stick and stay, in other words, I want students to graduate. I have proven strategies that help each student reach their educational and career goals.

College Success Coach | Teen Mentor | Founder of Education on Purpose
Email: bcollegeprep@yahoo.com | Facebook: eopurpose

Bob Mackey is dynamic and caring professional who uses his gifts for inspiration and motivation to inspire young men and women to achieve success in life. Bob has spoken before over 40,000 youth and adults and developed successful programs for schools, clubs and organizations all over the South, which has led him to the founding of M-Powering Choices. Bob has worked with many notable community leaders such as City of Atlanta Mayor Kasim Reed; former DeKalb District Attorney J. Tom Morgan; Chairman of Fulton County John Eaves; Alicia Phillips, President of the Community Foundation of Greater Atlanta; David Johns of White House Initiative on Educational Excellence for African Americans, Former Vice Chair of Georgia Board of Regents Felton Jenkins, Vice President of Boys & Girls Clubs of America Loraine Orr; Executive Director of Atlanta CARES Brenda Coleman, and Robin Ferst, Founder of the Ferst Foundation for Childhood Literacy. He has also earned the endorsement of ESPN Reporter/ Author Mark Schlabach, R & B Singer Bobby Valentino, Producer Jon Siskel; NBA Professional Basketball Player Dwight Howard, NFL Player Willie Whitehead, MY BROTHER'S KEEPER, White House Initiative, and Be Someone Founder Orrin Checkmate Hudson.

Founder of M Powering Choices | Founder & Facilitator of Power of the Knot, the Power of the Purse | Motivational Speaker | Author | Youth Mentor | Website: www.mpoweringchoices.net | Email: propersonalities@gmail.com | Facebook: mpoweringchoices

CRYSTAL SCRETCHING

Crystal Scretching is a dreamer. A native of the small town of Bay Saint Louis, Mississippi. Ms. Scretching never allowed what she saw in her environment to shape the imaginations she held in her mind. Equipped with a spiritual foundation set by her parents, and a creativity and passion for art, she ventured to college at the University of Southern Mississippi where she earned her Bachelor of Arts degree in Advertising and Graphic Design. Crystal Scretching is a proud mother, online marketing consultant, contributing writer and Founder of MyWallofDreams.com. Her passion is to inspire the world to follow their dreams, develop positive mindsets and spread self-acceptance.

Founder of My Wall of Dreams | Online Marketing Consultant | Contributing Author
Website: www.mywallofdreams.com | Email: crystal.scretching@gmail.com |
Facebook: MyWallofDreams | Twitter: CScretch | Instagram: CrystalScretching |
YouTube: MyWallofDreams | Google+: +CrystalScretching

42710066R00126

Made in the USA
Charleston, SC
06 June 2015